a simpler faith

Ed has lived in the trenches with people who have become injured or disillusioned with professional religion. He calls everyone to return to the heart of faith which was the part of our spiritual lives that resonated in the first place. *A Simpler Faith* will make you laugh, cry, and long for renewal.
—*Brian Boone, Senior Pastor, Edmonds, WA*

Ed Galisweski helps us see how we've overcomplicated something that should be simple and pure—our faith journey. With a call to focus on bringing believers back to God, Ed's "view from the pew" is funny and also seriously committed to helping the reader reconnect and simply focus on God and His promises and goodness.
—*Wayne Hastings, The Wayne Hastings Company, LLC*

Pastors, this is not a feel-good book. This is not a doctrinal treatise. This is a distress letter from Joe Public, asking hard questions from the pew. Prepare yourself. You will not agree with everything. You will be challenged by much of it. But you will be compelled to hear what our loved ones in the pew are saying.
—*Skip Rice, Director of Development/Morning Host, Power and Light Radio, KTLF-Light Praise*

Ed Galisewski has written a book that reflects the cry of his heart. He longs for Christians who've been damaged in churches to find healing and a way back to their God who is their Creator, Savior and Guide. Lamenting the fact that the Church is too divided, Ed calls for Christians to humble themselves and come together around the cross. *A Simpler Faith* will be a welcome encouragement to people who find themselves, for whatever reason, estranged from their church, angry at God, and not sure how to heal."—*Rev. Duane Cory, Sr. Pastor, Deer Creek Church*

"Something's missing, but I don't know what it is!" That's the nagging question that many believers have deep in their souls. Their faith is real, they want to grow but somehow feel a sense of flatness regarding their local church. Ed Galisewski in his book, *A Simpler Faith*, gives voice to the questions that will resonate with those serious about their journey of faith and looking for something more"—*Harv Powers, Ph.D., Licensed Clinical Psychologist – Leadership Consultant*

My friend, Ed Galisewski pretty much hits the nail on the head when he describes the 'man made add-ons' that infect nearly every established church group. In *A Simpler Faith* he suggests that it is possible to keep these infectious human systems from becoming tools that the enemy uses to divert God's wonderful intention for the function of the Body of Christ. Ed suggests a simple standard to which all churches ought to consider as their core. When we stick to the absolute basics we are empowered to be our real selves, encouraging others to discover God's love and mercy, and church becomes a safe place for worship, healing, giving and receiving all that the Lord has for His people!
—*Randy Northrup, Ph.D., Marital and Family Therapist, Pasadena, California*

I so appreciate Ed's candor, directness and vulnerability in taking on this subject! He says what needs to be said and provokes healthy thought. This book will causes us to take a look at our current state of worship in an honest and sincere way.
—*Paul Meriweather, CEO, PurpleNewt.Com*

a simpler faith

HOPE FOR PEOPLE WHO STRUGGLE WITH CHURCH

a simpler faith

Copyright © 2012 Ed Galisewski.
All rights reserved.

Published in association with Samizdat Creative
samizdatcreative.com
Editorial direction and interior design by Caleb J Seeling
Cover design by Jarrod Joplin

Illustrations by Drew Litton
www.drewlitton.com

Unless otherwise identified, all Scripture quotations in this publication are taken from the *Holy Bible, New International Version*® (NIV®). Copyright © 1973, 1978, 1984 by International Bible Society. Used by permission of Zondervan. All rights reserved. Other versions used include: the New American Standard Bible® (NASB), Copyright © 1960, 1962, 1963, 1968, 1971, 1972, 1973, 1975, 1977, 1995 by The Lockman Foundation. Used by permission; *THE MESSAGE* (MSG). Copyright © 1993, 1994, 1995, 1996, 2000, 2001, 2002. Used by permission of NavPress Publishing Group; and the *Holy Bible*, New Living Translation (NLT), copyright © 1996, 2004. Used by permission of Tyndale House Publishers, Inc., Wheaton, Illinois 60189. All rights reserved.

ISBN 978-0-9833280-2-5

To Louie and Michael,
my father and brother.

Two men who struggled
with the complexities of religion.
I write this in remembrance of you both.

Till we meet again.
—Eddie Boy

contents

Acknowledgments 13
Preface 15

part one
THE HUNGER FOR A SIMPLER FAITH

1. At the Foot of the Cross—In the Ramada 24
2. What Exactly Are We Offering? 31
3. Are They Off Base? Or Are We? 39

part two
SIGNS OF A SIMPLER FAITH

4. There Is God's Word—And There Is God's Touch 46
5. The Nature of the Fight—But Which Fight? 54
6. What If We're All a Little Wrong? 62
7. God Without the Baggage 68
8. Three Little Letters: C-S-G 73

part three
HOW A SIMPLER FAITH SHORT-CIRCUITS

9. The Nagging Problem of Other People's Faith! 82
10. Catholic Boy—In Paradise? 86
11. A New Set of Rules 91
12. Six Men—And a Boy 95

part four
THE URGENT NEED FOR A SIMPLER FAITH

13. Hitting the Adolescent Ceiling 102
14. Great Starts and Real Moments 109
15. Men—In a Spiritual Soup Line 116

part five
CHURCH BARRIERS TO A SIMPLER FAITH

16. Setting the Table—And Stacking the Deck 124
17. Doin' the "Corporate Creep" 129
18. The "Basting" Principle 136
19. Standing on the Word—But Whose Word? 140

part six
ACTING ON A SIMPLER FAITH

20. Making Like Toto—Pulling Back the Curtain 146
21. We're Off to See the Wizard! 151
22. Resisting the "Messiah Complex" 154
23. An "Audience of One" 157

part seven
THE CALL FOR A SIMPLER FAITH THROUGH HISTORY

24. Unity—A Rare Picture in History 164

25. The Runaway Conga Line 170
26. Landing in the Sandbox 179
27. From Transactions to Relationships 189

part eight

MOVING FORWARD TO A SIMPLER FAITH

28. Looking Around the Banquet Hall 200
29. Free in Christ!—Kinda 209
30. Facing Down Our Fears 214
31. Taking the First Step Toward
    the Good Things to Come 220

part nine

REFORMING A SIMPLER FAITH

32. The Most Powerful Witness 230
33. Options for a Simpler Faith? Oh, Yeah 239
34. A Helping Hand—from Pastors 247
35. In the House of Broken Dreams 256

part ten

A SIMPLER FAITH AS A CHRISTIAN WITNESS

36. And Our Worst Enemy Is 264
37. "Please, Not the God of the Bible!" 272

part eleven

PUTTING A SIMPLER FAITH TO WORK

38. Reengaging: It All Starts Here 282
39. Old Place or New? 288
40. Can You Dig It—Preacher? 293
41. Simple—From Cradle to Eternity 300

acknowledgments

First and foremost I want to thank my wife and children. Lynette, Braun, and Bryn have put up with my rantings for over five years. They have endured hundreds of hours of lecturing and explaining my side of this subject, so I could selfishly hone down the concepts in this book. They truly have put up with more than family should to appease their obsessed husband/dad.

Special thanks to Lynette for being my initial editor. Her efforts brought the first manuscript up to a readable level (not joking here). Tyler Waite thankfully reworked it with legitimate structure, and Caleb Seeling brought it across the finish line.

My writing partner and kindred spirit in this project was Scotty Sawyer. At times it seemed like we were of one heart and one mind while we were building the outline and storyline. His writing ability was what I prayed for and thankfully what I was blessed to find. It was overwhelming to research the book with him and find so much hurt and pain that was associated with church stuff. We both knew we had to attempt to bring some relief for those who have been disconnected from Christian community.

I have had many small groups over the years, but my current group has been pivotal in shaping the concepts in the book. I am blessed to have Darryl H (aka Hud), Keith T, Michael S, Tripp Y, David S in my life. This group has been a place of honesty and most importantly, a place to be broken and real.

Many thanks to the personal friends and clergy who have done some pre-reading for me to help me stay focused and clear. They made sure I was standing on solid ground, Biblically. These individuals gave me blunt feedback and helped me make the book more appropriate for all and therapeutic for those who are hurting.

My son Braun has been an inspiration for me through this journey. He struggles where I struggle and we had long talks on how to make this very readable for his generation. The current 18-25 year olds involved in faith are having a hard time digesting what my generation is feeding them. I thank him for being real and willing to ask the hard questions that so many are fearful to pose to their parents. Your mom and dad are thankful that you let us in to help you in that arena.

Special thanks to Drew Litton and his amazing talent. Drew has been treating Colorado residents for twenty years with his thought provoking satirical cartoons in the *Rocky Mountain News*. He has the ability to take an issue and synthesize the concept to a single frame and say more in it than some people need a page to write about. I went to Drew to get some names of people in his industry to make up cartoons for the book. After sharing my idea, he wanted in because he also has been struggling with the current direction of religion in America. I was so happy to have him on board and touched by the kindred spirit he had in this area.

And last, but not least, I want to thank God for putting this issue on my heart. He has taught me patience during the process of writing this book—a virtue I will continue to work on.

For your glory, Lord—not mine.

preface

Most people who write a book will ask a friend or colleague—usually somebody who's written a book themselves—to be the one to wax eloquent about the virtues of what the reader holds in his hands. I do not have that luxury. I have never written anything worth much up to this point in my life. (You'll be the judge of what is written here.) Nor do I have close friends who have published work. I just don't roll with that type of crowd.

Yet those minor things have nothing to do with why I feel so strongly about the goal of this venture. The book I've written is an attempt to bring comfort to people who have walked away from church. For years I've carried in my heart the pain of those who have a faith in God but have been disappointed by and disconnected from the institutional church. These believers now stand on the outside looking in—but it never should have come to this.

What qualifies me to speak on this subject? Good question. I'm missing the theological training that comes with a seminary degree. I'm just a guy who has watched church "happen" from the pews for the past twenty years—and I've identified an unhealthy pattern. (I've also got more than a decade of experience in lay ministry—and that has confirmed what I'm seeing.)

I term the pattern I see "manmade additions to the faith." These "additions"—standards, practices, and allegiances supposedly created for our spiritual benefit—have had the opposite effect.

Instead of drawing people closer to the Cross of Christ, these add-ons have overshadowed the meaning of the Cross. They have overcomplicated things. And they've scattered believers from the one place where we have all meaningful things in common: *the foot of the Cross*. This is the one place where together we can bring glory to God, as a body united under his headship. Yet sadly, as you look around at the Christian landscape, it's usually the last place we're found together.

Years of Perspective, Stacks of Research

I've spent several years examining this topic. And I've gathered information from a wide range of reliable sources within the Christian tradition. To me, there's a clear conclusion: These manmade additions are at the core of the growing disconnect between believers and the institutional church in America. The add-ons, more than anything else, have led to the alarming rate of disenfranchised believers who are abandoning the church in record numbers.

Recent research is bearing this out. Authors Robert Putnam and David Campbell have compiled studies on the seismic shift that's occurring in their book *American Grace: How Religion Divides and Unites Us*. They tell us Christians under thirty-five years of age want nothing to do with denominations. They don't want any connection to the add-ons that have separated believers for centuries. In short, our children have learned from our mistakes—and they're going in a different direction.

The question for us is clear: How do we right the ship?

You can judge for yourself whether a book like this should only be authored by someone who's deemed theologically astute. I say the shelves are already lined with books by those folks, and they say little or nothing about this problem. Sadly, some of those authors actually perpetuate the problem of manmade add-ons. In my opinion, they haven't stepped back far enough to get a clear perspective on the bigger problem.

That's where I come in. It's time for a "view from the pew." There has to be a place for a voice from someone like you or me—a Joe Palooka—somebody with a simple heart for God, representing those who suffer the most from our leaders' add-ons. Maybe at least one voice can offer insights from the ground level on the fracturing institution we call church in America.

Surprising Revelations, Energizing Hope
Maybe you know someone who has walked away from church—either for a short time (as I did), or who years later remains disconnected from a faith family. I think I can offer some hope. And some of the things I've discovered along the way may surprise you.

The easy conclusion—that the devil is at work trying to destroy the church—is true, but it's not the whole story. Of course the Enemy is at work doing that. But closer examination shows that much of the blame falls squarely on the shoulders of the church itself—on believers in God—and how our own devilish deeds have alienated other followers of God. Sadly, we've done the devil's work for him.

If you're one of the de-churched people I'm referring to, I hope this book brings you some comfort. I trust, too, that it rekindles hope in you for returning to a faith community. I offer practical advice—on *when to disengage*, for your own spiritual health, and *how to reengage* when your health is restored. Or maybe you know someone who has been disconnected from their faith. I hope this book gives some insight into why your loved one has taken a break from church—or possibly even rejected faith altogether.

Let me clear up a few things:

Don't expect this book to follow the norms of typical Christian literature. It won't. I don't aim to offend anyone, but my goal is to write to where the average Christian actually lives. (I'm going to write as if you and I are having a real conversation, full of real feelings—not the cleaned-up kind of conversation we think we "should" be having.)

Also, this book *won't* bring comfort to anyone who has walked away from faith with no intention of returning. If you're a diehard atheist—if you've "figured out" the universe and concluded there is nothing more than what you can physically see—then, please, hand this book to someone who still has questions. I didn't write it to win anyone back to faith. I wrote it to bring believers back to God.

However, if you're an atheist and you do decide to dip into this book, I expect that some of what I say will tick you off. I tackle some of the divisive issues that have plagued the church and that have given you plenty of fodder to make fun of believers. The church is at its most ridiculous when denominations try to prove themselves more right than others. This book is a biblically-based call for believers to begin acting in a more Christlike manner toward one another. As we become more Christlike, hopefully you atheists will have less material to mock us with—and may find your own path harder to embrace.

Who This Book Is For

At no other time has the church more needed a call to a simpler faith. And I've written this book with four types of readers in mind:

The de-churched man. This is the guy who has walked away from the church—and who may be slowly abandoning his walk with God. I'm talking about average guys who become fed up with church emphases they feel have nothing to do with

God. I'm convinced this number of men can't be counted.

I've spent years in ministry to men. And I've found that if a man is not engaged in spiritual community—if he's left alone with no spiritual connection—he slowly drifts away from actual faith in God. For women, it's a bit different, for various reasons. But this is the pattern for men. Eventually, they stop believing, if only because they've stopped talking about their faith, engaging it or growing in it. If they've left the church but still believe, their vibrant relationship is often just a gasp away from death.

I want to offer these men hope. I believe there is a way back to Christian community for the de-churched man who still has faith in God but is turned off by a church that seems to him irrelevant in addressing real life.

The content Christian. These are believers who are satisfied with life in their faith community. Like it or not, these Christians, however faithful, have become a part of the problem. One reason they're content is that they're happy to serve as "champions for the cause of Christ." Yet often there's a thin line between confident belief and a kind of certitude that borders on arrogance. I'm talking about our tendency to think we have things figured out (especially for others) and to fancy ourselves as the caretakers of God's truth. Rather than being righteous standard-bearers, we unwittingly erect barriers to those seeking God's grace.

Third, I hope to kick **all lazy believers** *in the butt and get them engaged again in a life of faith.* (Be honest—you know who you are.) These are Christians who go through the motions of faith but have a very nominal relationship with God (often as an entire denomination). They tend to be critical of the zealous crowd but have little to show for their own faith. Over time, their belief in Christ has gone from vibrant to nearly irrelevant. I want to challenge these readers to return to the deeply-lived faith they once had. And I want to examine how this group and the zealous "content Christians" may meet in the middle to unify, rather than being constantly at odds.

*Finally, this is a book for **ministers**—*those shepherds who care why men are leaving the church in droves or "checking out" even while they're in church. It's meant as a challenge to reexamine how things are done in our churches—and, more importantly, *why* they're done. Our practices and emphases may actually be turning people away from the communion they so desperately need. For that reason, leaders, you need to hear from those in the pews.

The main idea here is to examine why Trinitarian groups cannot and will not work together for God's glory. Their refusal to do so is counteractive to Christ's final prayer for his church before he submitted to the Cross. If we don't look at this problem clearly, we can't correct it. And if we don't correct it, we're sunk. It's not just atheists who are telling us this. It's our believing children.

The Power of a Simpler Faith

You'll realize early on, if you haven't already, that I'm just a simple dude. I'm not well-versed on deep theological points. (For that reason, I've had theologically trained readers scrutinize this book.) Yet I think you'll find that my "view from the pew"—and from behind the ministry curtain—can offer an advantage. It can illuminate important things we all need to get out on the table.

The most important of these is *the need for a simpler faith*. Man's add-ons have obscured the Cross and diminished its power. We have to put the cross of Christ front and center again—and I mean in a way that unites his followers rather than divides us. That breaks down barriers rather than builds them. It's the only way we will ever be one body, a united community of believers who love unconditionally and serve sacrificially. As you might imagine, putting the Cross front and center has eye-opening effects—on us and on the world.

So this is a book of hope for some and a challenge to others. Make no mistake, it's written to right some wrongs—and hopefully give believers a chance at community again. I believe that is God's heart. It will also sting some who read it—and it's intended to. In fact, some readers—mostly leaders—have a lot to lose by engaging the concepts in this book. I can safely say, that would be just fine with me. It'll be fine, too, with a whole lot of disenfranchised believers who are looking to reconnect with something genuine.

You might find some passages to be blunt or edgy, or some would say even vulgar (just as life can be!). But there is nothing in this book that mocks God. It only mocks the arrogant few who say they speak definitively for God. I don't have all the answers. But I am compelled to raise several questions that most people won't touch. These are questions that many believers want to ask but would rather sit in fearful silence than endure the consequences of raising them. Tragically, some of these people end up walking away from community—or even faith—rather than risk addressing their sincere concerns.

I think this is a book that no one has had the guts to write. That's the reason it's needed.

Ed Galisewski
(a.k.a. Joe Palooka)

part one

THE HUNGER FOR A SIMPLER FAITH

chapter 1

AT THE FOOT OF THE CROSS—IN THE RAMADA

> *After 2,000 years the Body of Christ is still dreadfully divided by doctrine, history, and day to day living. Scabrous stories about Christian disunity pepper the pages of periodicals and newspapers. The Body of Truth is bleeding from a thousand wounds.*
> —Brennan Manning, *The Ragamuffin Gospel*

It was approaching midnight, and we had argued for two hours. My roommate at this sales conference was a member of a church that most evangelicals wouldn't consider a part of orthodox Christianity. Me, I'm a hybrid evangelical-Catholic. We both were devout followers of our religious faiths. And we each had spent those last hours of the day telling the other guy exactly where he was off base. Honestly, we stopped only because we had to get up early the next day for a business meeting.

Neither of us was winning; we had just gone around and around. One guy would point out Scripture passages that validated his position. Then the other guy brought out his big guns, using the Bible to make his point. On and on it went, until finally it ended in bickering.

Now we sat in awkward silence. And I wondered: *Does anyone ever win at this stuff? What's the point?*

The point for both of us was simple: *It was to win the other guy over to our way of thinking.* What drove us was being more right than the other guy. It was to get him to see how wrong he was and to get him to change sides. So my roommate threw his denomination's distinctives at me, and I threw mine back at him.

Actually, he said things I'd never thought about before. And I took my turn to enlighten him about things he hadn't considered. But each of us remained convinced, "I'm right. Surely he can see my rules are better. Mine just make more common sense."

Two hours later we'd gotten nowhere.

Unmovable Beliefs and Sex Fantasies
Now we sat facing each other, embarrassed. And I began to feel wrong about the whole thing. In fact, I felt convicted by God. At the center of our debate was which guy's theology was the more correct take on salvation and the path to heaven. But now God's Spirit was hammering me about something else—something that obviously was more important to him.

Over the previous few days, I had sat through most of our sales meetings fantasizing about a woman there. I was having fierce mental battles, and I had to admit I wasn't winning any of them. I'm so weak when it comes to sexual desires that I often end up ashamed. I've never been unfaithful to my wife, but like many men, I've lost the struggle with lustful thoughts too often to keep count. The reality is, I'm just one more guy suffering from the "curse of the 'nads."

I knew I was nothing more than a common sinner. When I recognized that, I broke the awkward silence.

"Listen, buddy," I said. "I'm a hypocrite." I began to open up about my struggles. "I've been talking to you about all this theological stuff. But, really, when you get down to it, all I know is this: I lusted my way through that sales meeting today."

My roommate gazed at me as if he'd been hit with a two-by-four. No sooner had I gotten my confession out than he broke down and wept. Once he gathered himself, he admitted, "I've been having the same struggles." He'd acted as though he were doing fine, he said, because of a pressure he felt to put on that kind of front.

Here's the ironic thing about our debate that night: It had to do with how "our theology" led to some higher level of spirituality. We'd taken turns telling each other why our way, and our church, helps make godlier people.

Now we were humiliated. We wondered aloud, "What have we been doing these past two hours?" We knew we should just shut our mouths.

It was a cathartic moment—of guilt and shame, of conviction and repentance. In short, it was about what happens for every person at the cross of Christ:

Confession. Forgiveness. Freedom.

In that moment, my new friend and I set aside our doctrinal differences. We didn't need doctrine—*we needed healing*. And we ended that day with a renewing, refreshing time of blessing from God.

We knelt together, figuratively, at the foot of the Cross. It was the only place for either of us to be.

Crying Men and Common Worship

That powerful moment was an instructive one for both of us.

A bond had formed between us that cannot be broken. That bond is our complete indebtedness to the saving, cleansing, forgiving gift of Jesus Christ. We were united in our need for a

Savior—and also in our gratitude to him. When we saw what needy sinners we were, *all the theological points we'd been debating became meaningless.* They meant nothing, zero.

We realized, too, that what we had in common was more important than our differences. And what we had in common was the cross of Jesus Christ. Therefore, the best thing we could do was to *kneel together in common worship.*

I want to say something bold here: The same is true for all who claim to have a Christian faith. *Kneeling before the cross is the best any of us can do—not just on some days, but every day.* We all start out at the foot of the cross every day. And it's where we end our day. Nothing can improve on that.

That, in a nutshell, is the point of this book. Everything I write here will revolve around this point: The *simplicity of the Christian faith,* and our sinful departures from it. The Cross is the "one thing," folks.

My new faith buddy and I knew all too well we'd just run into the same wall of sin that we had the day before. And tomorrow would likely be the same. But we have hope that we can overcome that sin because we are sinners saved by grace. So, whenever we find ourselves at the foot of Cross, we know that's exactly where we need to be.

In retrospect, the kind of mutual confession we shared that night *is easy.* It's freeing. There's nothing bad about it. So, why are we reluctant to do it in each other's company? Why won't we let our guard down, to bond at the most important place in all of our lives—*the foot of the Cross?*

Missing Each Other and Missing Christ's Prayer

I shudder to think my new faith buddy and I might have missed that important experience. I know it was a life-changer for him. And it had a deep effect on me—to the point I'm writing about it in this opening chapter.

I couldn't help wondering in retrospect: Why had we wasted all that time, when something else was so much more important? It took two hours of arguing back and forth before I could bring myself to admit, "I'm a freaking hypocrite." What causes us to build up that kind of resistance? And what do we lose in the meantime?

I'm convinced all kinds of pressures lead to the kind of barriers my new friend and I faced. Pressures that are self-inflicted, society-inflicted, and church-inflicted. I want to look at those issues in this book. And I want to talk about the things we can do to change them, as individuals and as faith communities.

Make no mistake: This book isn't some gushy call to ecumenical oneness, holding hands and singing "Kumbaya." When I talk about unity at the Cross, I'm talking about something difficult. I'm referring to the hard, daily decision we make to pick up our cross and follow Christ—*and actually do the things he tells us.* And one of the last things Jesus said before leaving this earth was that *we are to be one.*

That's right—Jesus' most pressing concern before leaving the earth was *our unity*. He was looking ahead, to every generation of believer. And as he prayed, he made it clear that our witness as his body in this fractured, messed-up, chaotic world would depend on *our love for another.*

Picture the scene. Jesus had his disciples gathered around him at the Last Supper. The time was near for him to go to the cross. That's when Christ offered this prayer:

> "My prayer is not for (these disciples) alone. I pray also for those who will believe in me through their message, that all of them may be one, Father, just as you are in me and I am in you. May they also be in us so that the world may believe that you have sent me. I have given them the glory that you gave me, that they may be one as we are one: I in them and you in me. *May they be brought*

to complete unity to let the world know that you sent me and have loved them even as you have loved me" (John 17:20-23, emphasis added).

Do you get it? Our witness as Christ's body of believing followers cannot be separated from *the issue of our loving unity*. That's the final word—literally—from the Master himself.

I'm going to refer to his prayer again and again throughout this book. And we're going to explore respectful ways to do just what our Lord calls for: to unite in love. I'm not saying that is done simply—it's not. We're prone to dividing and alienating one another in all kinds of ways. But *obeying* God is *always* simple. Not always easy—but *always simple*.

In short, we're being invited to *a simpler way* to bring about his desires on the earth. To see his will done on earth as it is in heaven. And the first thing this means is to stop the insane disrespect between our groups. It also means looking at healthy ways to build a loving, **unified** body for the glory of God on earth.

It's not as big a task as it sounds. After all, it starts with you and me.

One-Minute Reflection:

What pressures keep you from connecting with believers different from you?

What do you think Jesus would say to you about those differences?

chapter 2

WHAT ARE WE OFFERING?

Back to the Ramada. Still at the foot of the Cross.

I had made a new friend. But this guy's denomination and mine don't have much respect for one another. Both have a lot of different rules for adhering to faith. Some major, some minor.

Every believer has legitimate reasons for choosing a group with its distinctives. But anytime those distinctives come between us and our fellow believer at the cross, trouble has already started. I'll show you from God's own Word that this trouble amounts to disobedience in his eyes. It is nothing less than sin.

Since the time of Jesus, the church has continually splintered into groups over theological differences. And today, disunity among the various groups of Christ-followers is at an all-time high. Generations of believers have spawned an attitude of spiritual superiority. This has torn apart any possibility of a unified front for God.

It's an ugly picture of unhealthy faith. Can we blame the unbelieving world for rejecting our concept of God? Can we fault them for seeing our mutual disrespect as totally unattractive?

I once heard a powerful sermon on what Christian unity should look like. He said our loving communion together provides a "foretaste" of heaven. The pastor drew his message from Ephesians 4, in which Paul urges unity in the body of Christ:

> Make every effort to keep the unity of the Spirit through the bond of peace. There is one body and one Spirit—just as you were called to one hope when you were called—one Lord, one faith, one baptism; one God and Father of all, who is over all and through all and in all. (Ephesians 4:3-6)

Paul goes on in this passage to speak about how we believers should practice grace and interdependence with each other.

"Unity of the Spirit"—Sound Familiar?

Paul's challenge here has a familiar ring. It's a direct echo of Jesus' final prayer on earth: "May they be brought to *complete unity to let the world know* that you sent me and have loved them even as you have loved me" (John 17:23, emphasis added).

Jesus said it. Paul said it. Are we getting it? It's a crucial message we need to get. Simply put, *our unity as believers is the primary basis for how the world knows Christ is Lord.* Loving unity in the church becomes a "foretaste" to the world of what heaven will be like.

Now let me ask you: *Can you believe how badly we have messed this up?*

If what we have now in the church is a "foretaste" of what's to come, can you understand why non-Christians say "no" to the idea of heaven? Is it a surprise so many refute any concept of God because what they see is so dysfunctional?

If the present situation is the best we can do, then we've already failed. Tell me: When was the last time you saw two churches in your area kneeling together at the foot of the Cross, literally or figuratively? When did you last see different denominations loving, supporting, and praying for each other? When did you last hear two groups speak respectfully of the other?

Let's bring it a little closer to home. How about your church? When was the last sermon you heard about the importance of presenting to the world a picture of unity, grace, and interdependence, as Jesus and Paul urge?

It doesn't happen. Not often enough, anyway, to see Christ's prayer become a reality on earth as it is in heaven.

So, what's causing this dysfunction? Is it the devil? Sorry, but manmade religion is the root cause of the problem. It's our add-ons that have usurped true religion. We've made it easier and easier over the years to polarize each other. We're our own worst enemy when it comes to tearing apart the fabric of Christian community.

Withholding Help Instead of Extending It
My new faith buddy and I ended that night by caring for each other in a way I'm convinced all believers should do. We were there to bear each other's burdens.

Turns out his burden was heavier than I could ever have imagined. He confided to me, "Look, I've confessed my battles to you here. But I still struggle."

"We all struggle," I reassured him. "I wish we didn't, but that's part of life."

Yet I had no idea the extent of his battles. They went way beyond his struggle with sin. You see, for years he had beaten himself up over his lustful thoughts, because of something his congregation taught. Their theology was that if you abided by certain rules, life would be a certain way for you. You wouldn't struggle with certain things.

This obviously hadn't happened for him. In short, he wasn't

able to remove his sin nature, as his church taught was possible. He just wasn't able to suppress those things that come with testosterone. And because of his sexual thoughts, he felt like a failure—to God, his wife, his family, and his community. I'm sure the anxiety he felt over it drove him even further into his temptation.

This man had no one to confess to. He couldn't divulge his battles to anyone in his community. He would have been ostracized. So he had resorted to living a lie, covering up what most of us think of as simple human struggles. For years, he had been stuck in a world of having to pretend.

Struggles That Can Topple a Manmade Empire
Try to imagine a best-case scenario for this man. Let's say he was able to go to someone in his community. He could admit his struggle to, say, his pastor, or an elder or friend. If his confessors were honest, they would have to admit, "Listen, son, I struggle, too."

But was that going to happen? No way! There was a "spiritual structure" in his community—constructed by man—which stated that no person of faith should be struggling with sin. If somebody were to struggle legitimately, acknowledging that they have a sin nature, it would expose the group's theology as a sham. Therefore, the problem was placed on the believer, rather than on the theology.

The whole system was supported by the aloofness of the leaders. They never let on they had struggles of any kind. After all, if they showed vulnerability, the whole carefully built religious structure might unravel.

Let's face it—this kind of situation isn't unique to my newfound friend. In any number of churches—evangelical, mainline, or fundamentalist; Catholic, Adventist, or Mormon—it's safer to act holy, as if you've got it all together.

And that leads to a lot of sickness. It stifles your ability to deal healthily with your sin, your real human struggles. Simply put, it inhibits you from being you. *And God won't deal with anything but your reality. He won't apply his grace to something fake or pretend. You can't grow if you don't bring your real self, warts and all.*

I knew it was going to be hard for my new friend. He wouldn't be able to share with his family and friends the joyful moment we had just experienced. He had enjoyed a beautiful moment with his redeeming Savior—but there was nobody to tell it to.

That's where my journey with this book began. I wanted to try to understand why such sickness in the church is so widespread...how rigid faith causes so much disunity and alienation among believers...and why we rarely find each other at the foot of the cross, where we all belong.

Muzzle Your Questions

I looked at my new friend with sorrow. I urged him, "Try to think of someone in your faith community who cares about

Ed Galisewski

you. Would it be possible to go to that person and say, 'I need to reexamine some of our group's rules. I think I'm suffering because of it.'"

He told me he couldn't. "If I do that, it'll show I'm not following one hundred percent," he explained. "They'll look at me as a heretic. They'll say, 'You're either all in or you're not.'"

He simply couldn't do it.

I could. When I was younger, I had needed to do just that. The commonly held view about Catholics (and it's a mistaken one) is that we're thought to be "all-or-nothing" about Catholic rules and regulations. People think we're forced to buy into every element or else be considered a heretic. But, in fact, I was able to tell my family members, "I don't think I can buy fifty percent of this. So I'm letting go of it. And I'm keeping the fifty percent I believe is of God."

My family's response was, "Okay." There was no stigma for me to live down, no accusations of heresy. I'll forever be grateful for that freedom.

Years later, there also came a time when I had to say to my evangelical friends, "I've got to drop some of the dogma our evangelical group has. It doesn't seem right. I need to walk away from it." Their response was like my family's. They said, "We'll walk with you."

I honestly believe I am a better Christian, a more whole and healthy servant of God, because of those choices.

What We Can Offer—But Won't

My new friend didn't have that same luxury. He wasn't even allowed to state his case.

This guy couldn't say to anybody in his community, "I'm not questioning anything about the basics—about the Father, the Son, or the Holy Spirit. I'm only questioning some aspects.

Please, can I talk to you about the twenty-five percent I think keeps me from growing in Christ?"

But it wasn't going to happen. Because of the rigidity of his group, he wasn't allowed to let go of *anything*.

The next thing my new friend said floored me. "I can't walk away from my community," he admitted. "But, Ed, I want you to know I'm going to kneel at the foot of the cross every day. That's enough for me for right now."

I nodded. And I wept.

Then he told me, with sadness, "You can't tell anyone I've said any of this."

I understood why. This man had been honest with me. And I have no doubt he'll be honest with God. I pray for him to find peace every day, in spite of not having true fellowship—the open-hearted kind—with any of the brothers and sisters he loves. He has a form of community, and I'm thankful for that. But it lacks the transparency and honesty needed to give him the support that every faith community should give one of its own.

Tell me: Do we have something to offer this guy? Other than a similar hypocrisy in our own group?

What, exactly, are we offering?

One-Minute Reflection:

How often does your group associate or join efforts with another?

How supportive is your faith group of someone who's struggling with sin?

Are you free to expose your sin to others around you? Why or why not?

What is the effect on you of "bottling it up"?

chapter 3

ARE THEY OFF BASE? OR ARE WE?

You've met my new friend. You've heard his honesty. You've seen his need. You know his dilemma.

Now I'll ask you to be honest. What was your first response to his problem? Did you reflexively think, "Of course the guy ran into a wall. He's got the wrong theology to begin with. He joined the wrong group with all their wrong rules and regulations. They're not of God." Be honest, now. Was that your first thought? If so, let me challenge you with two things:

My new friend is a lover of Jesus. And Jesus cares for him, no matter where he is theologically.

What about your own group? What was in the fine print when you signed up? What rules and regulations did you not find out about till later? Years down the road, do you still struggle and feel guilty because of similar teaching in your church? Is what you hear preached from the pulpit relevant to your real, inner life? Your hopes, struggles, and desires? Is this how you imagined life with God would be at this stage?

You've seen what an emphasis on manmade rules has done to people. It's led to bondage rather than freedom. It's led to isolation rather than fellowship. It's caused division rather than unity. And it's alienated those who ultimately couldn't buy into it. Those people ended up walking away from fellowship—and, in some cases, from faith.

Tell me, what does your church offer a guy like my new friend? I'm sure they would greet him with open arms the first time he walked through the doors. But years down the road, when he's expected to be "mature," would they treat him the same way his church is treating him?

Here's an even more important question: What would you have to offer my new friend? You may have already answered that with your first response: "He needs the right theology. He needs to get on board in the right church."

But is that really what he needs? Seriously?

Before you answer that, consider this: Is "correct theology" what Jesus teaches us to offer hurting people? Is that what *he* did? No. He offered people a simple theology—and it started with simple belief in him.

Getting Down to It

We all have more in common than we have differences. The Cross tells us that. My buddy and I couldn't have been farther apart theologically. But we learned the reality of just how close we truly are.

So, why do we emphasize the differences? Why do we isolate ourselves from other believing groups? What are we afraid of? And what does this isolation say about our regard for Jesus' prayer?

This leads to deeper questions: How do we really feel, personally, about God's desire for his church to be unified? What's our problem, our hesitation to consider pursuing it? Why do we flinch at the idea of presenting to the world a glowing picture of communion?

The answer to this has many dimensions. And we'll get to them in this book. But I'll repeat here something you need to understand: *It starts with you and me.* It starts in a hotel room with a hurting fellow believer. Just as it did with me.

We owe it to God to unify for his glory. When we don't, the first thing we do is kill our wounded. Like my new friend. I pray his faith survives the road ahead. But his church may very well finish it off. There's a road leading away from church that's lit-

tered with dead faith. And it's not the road that did the killing.

The Lord himself has issued a call to believers of every Trinitarian faith—all who believe in the Father, the Son, and the Holy Spirit—to unify for his glory. He knows what we do to each other the further we get from his cross. We bring harm to ourselves and others.

The First Line of Stubborn Resistance
I once served on the staff of a big-box church. There came a time when I questioned some practices I thought were harming people rather than helping them. These practices had been basic tenets of the church for years.

Finally, they accused, "You're trying to take apart the church's foundations." I answered, "I'm not trying to take apart the foundations of the Cross. I'm questioning the foundations that man has built, *so the Cross can do its work.*"

My point is, nobody wants to be the one to rock the boat. This is especially true if you're entangled with church powers. That can happen when you're on staff and your paycheck depends on your agreement with the leaders.

I had little to lose from speaking up. I had declined to be paid by the church, because I made a comfortable living from my day job. But I've got close friends who don't have that luxury. And they've been let go after getting crosswise with church leaders over things they felt weren't right.

The threat is different when lay people start to question things—but it's a threat just the same. For my new faith buddy to speak up, he'd risked losing his entire faith community. And not just his own but his wife's, his children's, their entire spiritual family and identity. Questioning anything would have led to their being completely shunned. That family would have lost everything meaningful they'd ever associated with God.

That isn't just a shame. To all lovers of Christ, it should seem a crime.

My Final Question for You
Let me ask you one last thing: What did you sign up for when you came to Christ? Was it a life of being right? A life of having the correct theology? A life of thinking yourself and your church are better than the believers down the street?

No—we signed up for a life of sacrificial, unconditional love for God and others. In short, *the Cross*. Even the world knows that about us. And the Nobel Prize Committee knows it as well as anyone. That's the subject of the next chapter.

One-Minute Reflection

> Which of the four groups I mention here do you most identify with? De-churched, zealous and content, lazy, or minister?
>
> Do you feel uneasy about speaking up over church practices you disagree with?

part two

SIGNS OF A SIMPLER FAITH

chapter 4

THERE IS GOD'S WORD—AND THERE IS GOD'S TOUCH

I have my reasons for loving Mother Teresa.

I've already mentioned I'm a hybrid Catholic-evangelical. And I value many things Catholicism gave me growing up. I especially cherish several Christ-centered aspects of faith that got lost when I ventured into the evangelical world. But more on that later.

For now, I want to say that sainthood isn't an aspect of Catholicism I was ever really into. Yet sainthood has nothing to do with why I admired the little nun from Albania who loved her way to a Nobel Peace Prize.

Mother Teresa had already been famous for a long time when she decided to attend to HIV patients. I remember when she made that decision. It had a deep and lasting effect on me.

This was fairly early in the AIDS crisis. At that time, certain Christian leaders were predicting, "Wait till Mother Teresa goes in to see those people. She'll confront them about their lifestyle. After all, they brought this plague on themselves."

But something else happened. When Mother Teresa first entered a room with a dying AIDS patient, she stood beside his bed. As she looked down at him, kissed him and wrapped her wrinkled hands around his head. Then she cradled him in her arms and told him she loved him.

Mother Teresa didn't have a sermon for that dying man. She just embraced him for Jesus. This, I knew, was Christ-centered love. And her ability to embody it was simply off the charts.

I've always loved this woman, but not because I think she's a saint. I know she was a sinner, no better than me or my buddy in the hotel room. I loved Mother Teresa because I identified with her. She came so close in my mind to obeying *what Jesus actually said to do*—not some man-filtered version of what Christ said, as so many of us have settled for.

Feeling the Gospel Versus Merely *Hearing* It

Mother Teresa's example reminds me of something important: *The world doesn't need so much to* hear *about the love of God as to* experience *God's love*. When you think about it, much of the world has the information it needs to know about the gospel. What they lack is the *touch* of the gospel.

So the question becomes: Who will help the world *feel* the love of God?

That's what Christ's incarnation was all about. And it's what Mother Teresa embodied in her ministry.

Mother Teresa's example had long been embedded in my heart when I got a call from a manager I knew in the pharmaceutical company I worked for. This was the mid-1990s, and our company had just developed a new medicine. A sales force was being put together to market the drug, and the manager wanted to know if I would be interested.

"What's the new medicine for?" I asked.

"It's for HIV infection," he said.

"Wow, that sounds exciting," I said. "Yes, I'd be very interested in that area of medicine."

He paused. "I'm a little concerned about the patients you'll have to work with," he said.

"What do you mean?" I asked.

"A large percentage of HIV positive patients are homosexual," he said. "I know you have strong Christian beliefs. Will you be okay working with this group of people?"

"I would love to interview for the job," I told him. "Let's start the process right away." Then I hung up the phone—and broke down crying.

I was crushed by his question. He had jumped to the conclusion I would have a problem working with people in the gay community. If he assumed I had those kinds of feelings—if this was a typical non-believer's perception of Christians—then I wanted to do something to prove him wrong.

Less than six months before that phone call, my wife and I had a very emotional talk on this subject. We had grown uncomfortable with some of the attitudes within evangelicalism toward the gay community, especially gays who were HIV positive. The manager's comments proved to me that our growing discomfort was based in reality.

We had noticed that, in some pockets of the church, the rhetoric was starting to rise to an abusive level. Soon I began to see that attitude spill over into the mainstream church and become voiced on occasion. Finally, I knew we believers had crossed the line when someone carried a certain sign at a gathering of Christians who were rallying on some issue. The sign's message sent a chill down my spine: "God Hates Fags."

I know that message is not a sentiment shared across the whole spectrum of Christians. But it is a sad statement by a few yahoos who are convinced they know the heart of God. When I saw the sign, I was shocked. My first impulse, which thankfully

I restrained, was to yell at the holder: "God hates *you* for holding that freaking sign, you jerk!"

If that sales manager only knew how badly I wanted to show the gay community and HIV positive patients that not all believers harbor ill feelings toward them. I just wanted an opportunity to "do a Mother Teresa" and let them know I loved them. I was happy, even eager, to sell a medication that would hopefully make their lives better. And, along the way, follow the advice of Saint Francis of Assisi: "Share your faith unceasingly; use words only when necessary."

You don't have to talk to share the gospel with people. You just need to love them.

An Award for *Loving Unconditionally?* Given by *Whom?*

Eventually Mother Teresa was awarded the Nobel Peace Prize. Now think about that. A panel of world experts on the Nobel Committee gave a nun the world's most prestigious award—and for what? This little woman did nothing more than what the Scriptures command us: to love our neighbor unconditionally.

Mother Teresa herself seemed baffled by it. She said on occasion, "I have been given this wonderful prize. Yet I have done nothing more than what Christ asks of every believer."

However, by doing that one thing well—*loving unconditionally*—Mother Teresa stood out to the world as a powerful example. What a picture of the gospel of Christ. A tiny woman emerges from a tiny country, known mostly for its state-sponsored atheism, and she turns the world completely upside down—*with love.* Christ's unconditional love.

The world will never be the same because of Mother Teresa's example. She exemplifies the very notion of sacrificial love. Service to the poor will never be seen the same way again, even in the secular realm.

Imagine what it would mean to have just a thousand people

doing what she has done. Yet we have trouble naming just one person who's like her!

What We Evangelicals Do with Our Mother Teresas

I remember the day Mother Teresa died. I was in a car with three other men, driving to a staff retreat for our big-box evangelical church. When the news broke about the little nun's death, the guys in the car asked each other, "Do you think she's in heaven?"

I was stunned. I couldn't believe such a question would be on any Christian's radar. *Mother Teresa, not in heaven? What could possibly cause them to wonder such a thing? They actually think she might be facing the alternative—hell? Are you kidding me?*

I sat in silence, muted by my own shock. I hoped one of them would inject some sanity. Instead, the consensus was, "Well, we just don't know." They thought they were being generous by saying this.

I felt so out of place. All I could think was, "She was so much closer to God's heart than any one of us in this car!"

Why were these dedicated Christian men debating whether

Mother Teresa was in heaven? It was for one reason alone: *She wasn't an evangelical.*

I loved these guys. They were my friends. And yet the best I could think of them in that moment was, *These men are pastors—yet they can't see beyond the blinders of their own religious orientation. It has completely twisted their thinking!*

Right Thinking Versus Righteous Living

I'm sure they didn't know it, but my friends were acting exactly like the people that Jesus was always mad at when he was on earth: the Pharisees. This was the group with the correct theology but no human empathy. They had all the right answers but, according to Christ, they missed the point in everything. Jesus even told a parable to demonstrate how misguided they were: the Parable of the Good Samaritan.

The Samaritans of that time were suspect to all the other Jews. Today, Samaritans would be the equivalent of a group we would think of as a cult. They had questionable worship practices and beliefs that were unorthodox in the extreme.

Jesus' parable identifies two "righteous" people in the story: a priest and a Levite. Then Jesus does something surprising. He tells his audience that a Samaritan who shows up—a cult member!—was more like their heavenly Father than the two so-called righteous figures. Why? The Samaritan had helped a hurting stranger with genuine compassion, while the others passed by the stranger for "religious" reasons.

Consider the audience Christ was addressing when he told the parable. It was *the Pharisees*—the guys who prided themselves on believing the right way. Imagine how steamed they were when Jesus publicly called them out this way.

I think Jesus was also calling out my friends in the car on the way to the staff retreat. The question about Mother Teresa shouldn't have been, "Does she have the right theology to get to heaven?" It should have been, "Between her and us, who's more like the heavenly Father? Who comes closer to actually fulfilling Christ's commands?"

Even the nonreligious Nobel Committee knew the answer to that question. And they rewarded it.

A Lesson for Us in the Evangelical Camp

Let's face it. Most of our efforts in the evangelical church are to get people to *think like us*, not to *follow Christ's example*. We work so hard to get people to agree with our worldview. If only we worked half that hard to persuade others to *follow our example as we follow Christ*.

Jesus' lesson on this subject was clear in his parable. But we could also use thousands of lessons from history, to see how often we've ignored his parable—to the church's disgrace.

Our misguided dogmatism has wrought terrible divisions and erected barriers throughout the centuries. It may have led to some "conversions," yes. But it has also brought about a poisonous view that sees everyone outside our group as sinners condemned to die. In short, it's a view that could condemn *even Mother Teresa*.

It's this very attitude that originally caused Christ's church to split into different denominations. Those early splits were the result of disagreements over doctrines and dogmas. They in themselves were a disgrace to Christ's prayer for unity. But, believe it or not, they were not the worst alternative. Without those split-offs, many disagreements ended in persecution leading to death.

So, do you think the days of persecution between believing Christians have ended? Not even close. Look around today. Persecution manifests itself in the zeal to correct and direct others to *"the right kind* of life in Christ." It also manifests itself in a lack of love and compassion for those outside our particular group.

I've already stated my belief that the non-Christian world today doesn't need to hear more about God—as much as they need to *experience the love of God*. Yet, is that what the world sees among Christians today? Is it mainly the love of God? Or is it the disrespect of vying denominations?

It's time we talk about oneness. And, realistically, there's only one place that conversation can happen: *at the foot of the Cross*.

One-Minute Reflection:

> Does your faith group emphasize feeling God's love as much as hearing His Word?
>
> How would your faith group view a Mother Teresa?

chapter 5

THE NATURE OF THE FIGHT—BUT WHICH FIGHT?

You've heard Jesus' prayer for oneness. And you've heard spiritual leaders debate Mother Teresa's salvation. Feel a little dizzy? You should.

We're not exactly presenting a "glowing picture of communion" to a fractured world. As I've said, disunity amongst believers is at an all-time high. How can we expect the world to see unity among us when we don't see it ourselves?

It's obvious there's a huge split between believers in America today. And, if you'll excuse my sweeping generalization, most of us fall into one of two camps. See which one you might land closer to.

On one side are the traditional mainline denominations—the Old Guard—and all the history and precedents they bring with them. On the other side are the Newbies—the newer, nondenominational, mostly evangelical groups—which make up the newer wave of people of faith.

It's an understatement to say these two sides don't respect each other. The fact is, each side questions the legitimacy of the other's faith.

Newbies: On Patrol for God

In general, Newbies think they're far more spiritual than the Old Guard. Newbies disrespect the Old Guard to the point that they question whether they have faith in God at all. (Just as my friends in the car questioned Mother Teresa's faith.)

This aggressive group sees themselves as being on "God patrol." Their main energy is spent running around like meter maids, handing out citations to those whose claim to salvation is "insufficient."

Old Guard: Sitting on the Sidelines

On the other side of the barrier are the traditionalists. They're so disgusted by the Newbies and their overzealousness that the Old Guard do all they can to distance themselves.

But in the process, the Old Guard mute their own faith, going into a kind of shutdown mode. Rather than risk appearing too religious, they end up muzzling their own efforts to share the Good News. Before they know it, they've moved away from the Cross (just as the Newbies have accused them of doing all along!).

The Price of Sitting Back

The sad outcome of this feud—a bad action followed by a bad reaction—is that both sides suffer. Sure, the Newbies have become a kind of Gestapo for God. But we also can't underestimate how truly unspiritual many in the Old Guard have become.

What I'm about to say may seem like I'm picking on the Old Guard. Rest assured, I reserve most of my criticism in this book for the overzealous. Please keep that in mind as you read on.

Many in the Old Guard freely mock zealous Christians—and that's as spiritual as they get. They essentially stand on the sidelines tossing criticisms like so many beer bottles onto the field where the zealous players are engaged in real struggle. These vocal critics simply avoid the faith dialogue that Newbies have established with the world. Instead, the Old Guard hide behind their criticism because they don't have an adequate response to the Newbies' zeal.

If the Old Guard wants to tell the Newbies to shut up, they'd better be prepared to do something more than just stand on the sidelines and mock or critique what the Newbies are doing. They need to be willing to provide an example of grace for the Newbies to emulate.

Maybe you think spiritual laziness is just a "passive" trait. You shrug it off as a harmless "sin of omission." Well, I can tell you, there's a bigger danger to passive faith than you might think.

From Dissatisfaction to Zeal . . . to Silence

Because my heritage is Catholic, I notice a lot of trends in that arm of Christ's church. One such trend is that a surprising number of Catholics convert to Mormonism. Why? They see in Mormons a religious faith that's active and involved. It seems much more real to them than their Catholic faith.

In most cases, these Catholics' spiritual lives have been mundane for years. So, naturally, they're drawn to the more active Mormon church. Mormons are community-oriented, devoted to family, and zealous in evangelism. To Catholics, Mormons act on what they believe, and that has great appeal.

I know a guy who followed this very trajectory. He's naturally wired as a driven type of guy, and he grew up Catholic. What enticed him to Mormonism was the evangelistic aspect. He was excited at the idea of being able to say, "I brought so many people to the family this week." This guy loved getting people to commit to faith. And the Mormons' emphasis on missions, at home and abroad, had great appeal for him. Finally, he jumped in with total enthusiasm.

When I asked him about the dramatic switch he'd made, he was elated. He said, "Ed, Catholicism meant nothing to me. When I became a Mormon, I went on a yearlong mission!" He couldn't have been more thrilled.

A few years later, this same man walked away from the Mormon church. Over time, he had to set aside much of the church's theology, things he couldn't buy into. And because of that, he was no longer accepted by his new faith community. So he left altogether. He hasn't been in a church since.

In short, this guy had gone from "too little" to "too much"—and, eventually, to "nothing." Today he's one of a multitude of men who doesn't do anything in regard to faith. He's drifted away from belief completely.

A lot of evangelicals reading this will say, "That guy was better off having left. The Mormon church is way off base." But that isn't the question here. The question is this: *How many evangelical men follow the same trajectory?* They reject the mainline denomination of their childhood because to them it never stood for anything. Later, when faith ignites in them, they jump into a zealous evangelical church. But after a while, that zealous group's regulations start to wear him down.

Such a guy won't go back to the Old Guard. And the Newbies' manmade rules are draining the life out of him. So he can't stay where he is—but he doesn't see a way forward.

One day, he just stops going to church. And he never goes back.

Time passes, and some of his old zealous friends show up at his door. They tell him, "Hey, we finally saw the same problems you did. We're starting a new group and we'd like you to join us."

But the guy is skeptical. He's seen this same cycle time after time: Good people split off from their church and start a new group. But the new group only perpetuates the old problems. Pretty soon people are wandering away, looking for their next stop on the faith tour.

He's tired of it all. His trust level has been worn down to nothing. So he stays put, away from church. And, eventually, away from God.

Tell me—can you blame him?

A Way Forward

One of my hopes for the church is that believers on both sides of this divide—the Old Guard and the Newbies—will decide enough is enough. They'll see the need to connect—to set aside their petty differences for God's glory—and to worship and work together as one for him. They'll pool their collective energies and humbly unite at the foot of the cross.

To you believers in the Old Guard, I say, Stop allowing yourselves to be marginalized. Renew your excitement for God! If you have an authentic relationship with God through Christ, state it and be proud of it. Don't let your stubbornness silence you. You've been given the gift of salvation, and that gift is meant to be shared. Only you can make that happen, through the power of God's Spirit.

To us in the Newbie camp, I say, Everybody, check your arrogance at the door. Jesus makes clear he has no room for it. *Show* God's love first—*then* offer his Scripture. God's words will always have a stronger impact if you demonstrate his love with genuine self-sacrifice. That's the way of the Cross.

We two groups are not as far away from each other as we might think. But it's a constant battle to keep our sinful nature from getting in the way of God's intention for our fellowship.

Who Gets Pushed Out of the Way in All This?

The guy who gets lost in all this denominational bickering is the marginalized man. I'm talking about the average guy—Joe Palooka—who loves God and hasn't lost his faith. He wants his life to count for the gospel—but doesn't see anywhere to do this without attaching himself to some denominational nonsense.

This guy wants nothing to do with the inconsequential crap he sees in church life. Day by day, he grows more frustrated by the nonsense-makers who are calling the shots, making church seem less and less relevant to the reality he knows. Now he, too, is on the verge of quitting it all. *Yet all he wants is a simpler faith!* To me, this guy is reason enough to set aside our differences. He alone provides motivation to join those on the other side and kneel together in common worship. As Paul says, *There is one body and one Spirit. And, yes, even one baptism!* (see Ephesians 4:4-5). He's telling us, *Listen, you make a big deal out of whether to sprinkle or dunk. But it's all the same in God's eyes. Your unity is meant to be a foretaste of heaven!*

Where is this foretaste seen most clearly? *At the foot of the Cross.* It's there, in between these two groups, Newbies and Old Guard, that the true work of the gospel has the greatest impact. But instead, we stay polarized, stifling God's desire for his kingdom to appear "on earth as it is in heaven."

The time has come for the world to see—indeed, to feel—what we in the body of Christ are meant to experience and express together: *the love of our Lord and Savior.*

The Joy of Being Wrong!
It's time for the lazy believer to find his fire again. It's also time for the zealous believer to readjust his focus—from *being right to having compassion.* And it's time for both sides—and the ministers who lead them—to help bear the burden of the drifting man. We need to draw Joe Palooka back into the fold. To bring him hope and guidance on how to reengage his faith in a healthy way. And to remove all the pressures that caused him to check out in the first place.

It's time we acknowledge, "I've always thought I had to be one hundred percent right in my theology and practices. But *every* Christian believes that. So . . . what if I'm just a little bit wrong? In fact, what if there is no 'right group' who has it all down? What if *we're all just a little wrong?*"

That's what we'll explore in the next chapter.

One-Minute Reflection:

Where do you find yourself in the war between Newbies and the Old Guard?

Do you know men who have sidelined themselves from church out of sheer futility?

chapter 6

WHAT IF WE'RE ALL A LITTLE WRONG?

The weight room at the gym was more crowded than usual on this Saturday. As I looked around, I saw several guys I'd befriended over the years. They were spotting each other, doing reps, clanking iron. I couldn't suppress a grin. In my Joe Palooka world, there is no sweeter sight and sound.

We all knew each other and had become a kind of informal group. In the southwest area of Metro Denver where I live, we were as varied a crew of workout buddies as you could get. Yet we were totally at ease with each other, in an environment we enjoyed.

This Saturday I decided to step out and take a little risk. I wanted to start a discussion with these guys. Maybe even draw in strangers who might be interested. My topic was guaranteed to get the blood pumping quicker than any weightlifting routine.

Religion.

"Hey, guys," I called out. "Tell me about your religious upbringing. How does your faith group look at other groups?"

Jimmy the evangelical weighed in, swaggering with

confidence. He knew I was of an evangelical-Catholic mix. He stated in very clear terms that he didn't believe people of my Catholic background were "saved."

Mike the Catholic stated just the opposite. He cautioned me that if I wasn't adhering to all the Catholic sacraments, I might be in jeopardy.

Tom the Lutheran jumped into the fray. He pointed out that Jimmy's faith was missing an all-important component: "Confirmation."

That caused Eric the Baptist to chime in. He told Tom that Lutherans lack the most important component of all: "A personal relationship with Jesus Christ."

Chuck the charismatic made a similar declaration about Presbyterians. He said his time in that denomination convinced him God's Spirit never attended their services—"if he's ever been there at all."

If other groups had been represented in that weight room, they surely would have pumped up their position. An Adventist would have instructed us on the proper day of the week to worship. A Mennonite would have told us which social issues were at the top of God's agenda—and which weren't.

Around and around it went. In the end, every guy had suspicions about all the others. Why not? Each of us had been taught by our denomination, in ways subtle and overt, that our group alone had the divine recipe. Only we and those like us had the proper concept of God—how to worship him, how to understand him, how to lead a life of faith. Down deep, each of us believed God was moving us to the head of the line quicker than anybody else.

Talk about arrogance!

It's this very attitude—one of exclusivity—that caused Jesus to ride the Pharisees so hard. Time after time in the gospels, Jesus called those guys out. He said their religious prescription for everyone didn't benefit anybody. Their rules didn't make people more righteous—in fact, they had the opposite effect.

Recognize Yourself in That Weight Room?
Be honest. Place yourself somewhere in that weight room, among us guys. Do you recognize yourself in anything that was said? Did you hear your own attitudes, or something resembling them?

Let's face it, we all think we're the only ones who are right. But how can that possibly be? How could there be one group tucked away in some corner of the world that has everything right?

Let me fill you in on a little secret. *We can't all be right.*

Some of the numbers are startling. Did you know that about thirty-four thousand different Christian groups have been started worldwide since the time of Christ (30 AD)? And that as many as twelve hundred exist in the US alone.[1] This is an amazing fact when you remember that they all originated from a single event. And each believes their way is a little better than the one down the street. Some even believe theirs is the *only* right way.

This arrogance has persisted through every generation since the church's beginnings. Everybody thinks *only their group* is right.

But it's not just denominations that make this claim. Deep down, many of us put great pressure on ourselves to be "right" in our beliefs. Otherwise, we fear we're personally failing God.

Now let me pose a different idea to you—something a little more realistic. Something that may even be in line with the Scriptures.

What if . . . *we're all a little bit wrong?*

---

[1] http://www.numberof.net/number-of-christian-denominations/ (accessed 8/25/2011)

Yet Another Dirty Little Secret

A magazine recently interviewed Randall Wallace, the guy who wrote the screenplay for *Braveheart, We Were Soldiers, Secretariat*, and others. Turns out Wallace went to seminary and said he learned something important there. It was this: *God's revelation to man is perfect. Man's expression of God's revelation is imperfect.*

Pretty simple, huh? You would think an idea like that might benefit us all. It might bring some freedom—as in, it's okay to be a little bit wrong. So, why are we so uncomfortable with it?

To answer that question, let me share another little secret with you. All those guys in the gym? The ones who righteously picked apart each other's faith? *Very few of them actually go to church.*

That's right. These guys know their denomination's distinctives very well. They're experts on the finer points of their group's theology. Yet for all that knowledge, very few of them have *a home for their faith*. From the sound of them, you'd think these guys adhere to everything their denomination teaches. Yet, in reality, none of those guys has found a suitable home for his faith. So, why the disconnect? How did it happen? Where, exactly, did things break down?

It turns out these guys are just a small microcosm of a larger phenomenon. To get to some kind of answer, we need to see what's happening in the bigger picture.

People Are Choosing Not to Stay

Not long ago, a statistic on my home state of Colorado grabbed my attention. It revealed that only fourteen percent of people living in Colorado attend church.

I had to wonder about that. Does this mean only 14 percent of Coloradans are Christians? And, if so, does that mean 86 percent are agnostic or atheists?

Of course not. Polls show that Coloradans' religious beliefs are roughly the same as the national trend. And the overwhelming majority of Americans state a belief in God. (At last count, that number was well above 80 percent.) In fact, the vast majority go so far as to claim they're "born again." So the research leans much farther toward belief than toward unbelief.

Okay then, I thought. I'll accept that only fourteen percent of Coloradans attend church. Yet what does that tell us?

Are most people of faith here just lazy or negligent? That couldn't be, either. I, for one, had gone to church for years just for my family's sake. I felt a lot of pressure to make church work for my kids. And I know that a lot of guys are the same. They're willing to gut it up on most Sundays for their family's sake. So, in that respect, the fourteen percent figure still doesn't add up.

Okay. What about the call of the outdoors? Are Christians here more likely to spend their Sunday mornings on a mountain? Nope. Sorry to shatter the stereotype, but Coloradans still prefer a church sanctuary as their place of worship on Sundays.

Well, then—are believers in Colorado just more nonchalant about church than Christians in other places? I've got news for you: Christians here are no different from anywhere else. It doesn't matter where you live. If you identify yourself as a follower of Jesus, at some level you take that seriously. People don't lose their convictions as soon as they move to Colorado and get a look at the Rocky Mountains. If anything, it inspires them *toward* God!

Fourteen percent. It's a head-scratcher, all right. Yet there it sits before us—a puzzling and startling fact: *The vast majority of Christians in Colorado choose actively and deliberately not to go to church.*

What could possibly be at the root of this decision?

Here's an even bigger head-scratcher. *It's not just Coloradans. It's happening everywhere.*

Tracking the Masses of Disillusioned Believers

You've got to ask yourself. Could it be that these de-churched people—believers who state a Christian faith—feel disconnected from organized religious groups?

In other words: Are my guys at the gym indeed a reflection of a larger problem? Why *do* people give up on church? (Or do churches give up on them?) What makes them turn away?

One thing is clear. Denominational distinctives don't keep people in church. You can conveniently fall back on doctrine when you're in a conversation about religion—just as my guys did. But when the real issues of life hit you, those things just don't cut it. People need something more. Or, more accurately, they need something *more real*.

I've found a lot of clues to the answers we're looking for. Where, you ask? In the one place where people speak most freely, except for maybe a confessional.

An airplane seat.

One-Minute Reflection:

> Do you hear yourself in any of my buddies' comments in the gym? What was it like to hear all their doctrinal divisions aired in public?

> Deep down, what really makes you afraid of being just a little wrong?

chapter 7

GOD WITHOUT THE BAGGAGE

I'm one of *those* guys.

In my job as a pharmaceutical rep, I travel a lot. And, yeah, I'm the guy in the seat next to you—the one who always strikes up a conversation. Here's the typical scenario, and it rarely varies.

When the flight takes off from Denver, I've already been chit-chatting with the guy I'm sitting next to. Soon I've waded into a little casual conversation. "So, how are things going for you?" I ask.

We have the common exchange about each other's stresses and strains. Just comparing notes on the usual challenges of life. Then, when it seems appropriate to leave the shallow end of the pool, I'll ask: "Do you mind if I ask you what role God has played in your life?"

The guy is usually guarded at first. Anyone would be. But, gradually, he begins to share his thoughts. And this includes a lot of disillusionment over God and religion.

It becomes clear pretty quickly that he isn't asked this question very often. Because suddenly the guy is not just willing but eager to pour out his thoughts on faith—even to a stranger like me.

Fifteen Years of In-flight Data
Over the next two hours, the conversation we have is like hundreds of others I've shared in fifteen years on the road. Believe me, there is very little variation in these stories. In fact, the majority are so similar it's eerie.

The men who tell me their stories usually fall into one of two categories:

First, there are men who are actively engaged in church life—but they're disillusioned over the rules and regulations of their particular group.

These concerns aren't serious enough to lead them away from church. But they continue to be nagged by questions that never get answered. They struggle over meaningless rituals and add-ons that distinguish their denomination. "Why are these things considered 'essentials'?" they wonder. "And why am I doing them? Why does it feel like none of this has anything to do with following God?"

Second, there are men who are de-churched at present because of some past disillusionment with their faith community.

At some point, these guys walked away from their religious roots. And they carried with them a lot of unresolved baggage. Their concerns were never addressed within their church. Now, years later, those concerns still haven't been processed. The men in this category have no plans to reengage with a faith community in the future.

Always a Story—and It's Usually Heartbreaking
What strikes me most about these conversations is that behind every one is a flesh-and-blood story. And it's usually a tragic one.

For whatever reason, the guy has become disconnected from his faith community. In turn, he disconnects from his own deepest questions about life—and any source of answers.

I can't tell you how deeply these conversations have tugged

at my heart. Some have *broken* my heart.

After fifteen years of listening, I'm more impassioned than ever to connect with these men. Each time I encounter one, and his disillusionment comes pouring out, I want to offer him something real. I want to talk to him about a way he can love God again. I want to offer him a way of living out his faith that touches all points of his life. I want him to be able to draw on a simple faith—one that's minus all the disappointments and distractions that burdened him before.

I know of which I speak. Because I'm one of those guys. I've been where they are.

After hundreds of such conversations—all of them involving a trail of disillusionment—I started to wonder: "Why is this the experience for so many men? This conversation never seems to change. All these guys are alienated. Why does the pattern continue? And what can be done to reverse it?"

Three Universal Complaints

I've learned something very telling from these conversations. That is, both groups of men—those engaged or disengaged with faith—have the same complaints! All these guys share the same objections and struggles over practices in their faith community. I've boiled these negatives down to three primary areas:

There are too many *manmade add-ons* in their group's expression of faith. These things may add "distinctives" to their denomination. But in practical terms, they detract from a person's experience of God. Man always wants to add a little more to the recipe—and there's a danger in that.

Power structures exist within their faith group. This often ends with the pastor's agenda taking precedence over God's. At first the emphasis was on doing the works of the Lord. But soon the emphasis becomes a drive to sustain the church itself (or the pastor's personal goals).

There is an obnoxious *arrogance among the faithful*. Believers' "rightness"—and their ready prescriptions for others—do incredible harm. Instead of helping others connect with God, these zealots have a draining effect because of their judgmental approach.

Simply put, what these disconnected men want is *God without the baggage*.

And that's exactly what I want for them. My desire is for every disillusioned man to be able to have a real conversation about faith—one where no question is taboo and no personal

struggle is judged. One where God himself—Father, Son, and Holy Spirit—can again become the real focus.

A Prescription in Three Letters

There's an easy way men can do this. All the power of the universe—and power for their lives—can be summed up in this shorthand: *C-S-G*.

Ed Galisewski

One-Minute Reflection:

Are you disillusioned at times over the rules, regulations, and add-ons of your faith group?

What particular "baggage" most frustrates you about church life?

chapter 8

THREE LITTLE LETTERS: C-S-G

I've heard a lot of disappointment in these guys' stories. But I've also discovered powerful reasons for hope.

Ironically, both groups of men—the de-churched as well as those engaged with faith—express a common desire. *They all want a simple approach to faith.*

It's taken fifteen years of conversations for me to recognize the obvious. That is, there are three simple yet powerful elements to faith. Each one of these speaks to our everyday lives—because each one addresses one of the three Big Questions we all have about life.

Whenever I've presented these three basics to my seatmate on a plane, almost everybody could relate. And that includes the nonbelievers. Here's what I discovered about them:

1. *They believe in a Creator.* They know this world didn't come from nothing. The idea of a divine Creator makes sense to them. Most men said they believe in something more than the eye could see. They know there's a reality beyond their last breath.

2. *They acknowledge the need for a Savior.* They know they're

fallen creatures. And they freely admit their need for forgiveness, help, and hope. Most men are all too aware they're sinners. Their own "stuff" reminds them of it every day!

3. *They see the need for a Guide*—a living Spirit to empower them daily—to live, love, and serve beyond their ability. It's the rare guy who reaches out and asks for help. But that doesn't mean they don't want it. They realize they need a power beyond themselves to help them.

I've learned over the years to use this simple "C-S-G" approach—Creator-Savior-Guide—in talking with men. It almost always seems to hit the mark for them.

Even most de-churched men tell me they would consider reengaging with a faith community if it operated with this primary focus: our relationship with the Creator, Savior, and Guide. Of course, what we're talking about here is the Triune God—the Father, the Son and the Holy Spirit.

Not surprisingly, I found the same desire for simplicity among the church-going men I encountered. They were just as enthusiastic for this kind of back-to-basics faith experience.

How We've Moved Away from the Basics

So, how did we ever get away from this basic focus? Why did we abandon simplicity?

The main reason is a concept I've already mentioned: *distinctives*. These are things that are secondary to faith, but groups often make them a primary focus. Things such as *how you do baptism*. Does your denomination dip, sprinkle, or dunk? Believe it or not, some Christians believe their salvation is tied to a certain method of baptism.

What about communion? How do you take the bread: wafer, saltine, unleavened, oyster cracker, ripped chunk from a whole loaf? How about the cup? Wine or grape juice? Community cup, individual cup, "dunk the chunk"? Do you believe the elements

become actual flesh and blood, or that they represent a passionate sacrifice? Who is allowed to serve communion? Ministers only? Elders and lay people? Men only, or women, too?

Where do women have a place in your group? Pulpit preachers, pulpit announcers, pulpit anything? Elder or deacon board? Greeting and Sunday school teaching only?

Do you speak in tongues? Do you believe you have to have this gift, or that it's nice to have it, or that it's bad to have it? Are you a dispensationalist (That's a big fancy word, isn't it.)? Do you believe Christ's Second Coming will happen before or after the period of tribulation in the book of Revelation?

Do you meet for worship on Sundays? Saturdays? What is the "official" sabbath day, anyway? Do you know why?

All these things are denominational *distinctives*. And we each have the right to observe them however we think is right. Yet there's one thing we need to agree on about them, but we can't seem to: *They're all secondary to the core faith of Christianity.* All these things are important to faith, yes. But they're also *the underlying culprits for driving good men and women away from a basic focus on the Cross.*

Ed Galisewski

Not only that: We tend to discredit other believers—even their salvation—based on how they do these things. *Secondary* things. At times, distinctives are wielded like weapons. Some groups use them to force people into decisions that ultimately are no more important than the difference between Jif or Skippy peanut butter. Distinctives can even determine the ends of friendships. All because you chose to dip instead of dunk.

Centuries of Adding and Subtracting

For centuries, humans have used distinctives to add and subtract from God's message. It's a dysfunction that has existed since the time of Christ. Meanwhile, the problem multiplies with every church that splinters, with every offshoot from a denomination. And it has reached an apex today. All those non-churchgoing masses are proof of how dysfunctional we've become.

So how do we move forward in any fruitful way?

First, believers need the freedom, courage, and honesty to assess what is *spiritually essential* and *what is not*. That means looking squarely at the manmade elements in the church that have divided rather than united us. Only by looking at those historical patterns—from ancient to recent—can we see how manmade structures have intruded on God's plan. And maybe we can avoid the many pitfalls.

Make no mistake: This book is not a call for another denomination. That's the last thing the world needs. All too often, whenever we have an issue with some aspect of our denomination, we take it upon ourselves to start a new group fitted to our view of things. We simply add or subtract elements in order to meet our own needs.

Yet by creating more groups, we grow farther and farther away from each other—and from Christ's desire for us: "May they be brought to complete unity *to let the world know* that you sent me and have loved them even as you have loved me" (John 17:23, emphasis added).

Christ's desire is for us to worship as one body—and to love each other in a way that causes the world to watch in amazement. When we do this, our oneness—with each other and with him—broadcasts to the world the true loving nature of our God.

Reexamining All Through the Light of C-S-G

No matter where you are in regard to church, I want something important for you. I want freedom for every man who has walked away from church but still believes in God. Freedom to explore again the reality of a Creator, Savior, and Guide—and to let his faith journey develop from there. I want freedom for every rank-and-file believer to question certain elements of his or her faith group and not feel threatened about it.

And I want something for both types of men—churched or de-churched—all of whom have been turned off by manmade elements of organized religion. For all of these men, I want to offer a path back to real community in God.

It's time for zealous Newbies to examine their arrogance in light of a C-S-G focus. Likewise for Old Guard believers: They need to examine their resentment and passivity in light of C-S-G. Imagine what fellowship would look like between these two groups if they adopted a basic C-S-G approach. Wouldn't we come a lot closer to genuine, heartfelt unity if our focus was on our common faith in God through Christ, with the help of the Spirit?

I want something else for men, too. It's time for ministers to get actively involved in the discussion. Every shepherd of God needs to examine his own motives for emphasizing his denomination's distinctives.

For example, maybe you're a pastor who sees your church as "God honoring." If that's true, you should welcome a healthy critique on how well you approach the task of emphasizing C-S-G—the central role of the Father, the Son, and the Holy

Spirit in the life of every believer. As you progress through this book, I hope you'll keep asking yourself, "Does my leadership show a focus on C-S-G? Do I keep things simple for my people in their service to God, based on their relationship to the Father, Son, and Holy Spirit?"

With the cooperation of both of these groups—and the ministers who lead them—maybe we'll see the polarization diminish. And maybe we'll see fewer barriers between believers—and more energy toward God's will being done "on earth as it is in heaven."

Back to the Gym
Think back now to that scene at the gym. All that denominational bickering.

The truth is, when it comes to Trinitarian faiths, we're all pretty close. We have a lot more in common than differences. *Yet the differences dictate our attitudes.*

To me, it all comes from the top. I was involved in church ministry for years. And I saw the depths that denominational leaders would descend to, to entice believers away from other traditions. I saw the strategies they used to keep people under their roof. The rallying cry was, "A fight for souls!" But the motive was to expand their own flocks—to see their own numbers grow at the expense of another group.

Finally, it dawned on me. I realized, "What if a random group of men from different denominations got together? Say, a Catholic, a Methodist, a Lutheran, a Baptist, and an evangelical. If they started talking about their faith, they would *disagree* rather than agree. All because of what their denomination had taught them about the other. Yet they would have the basics—the very foundations of the faith—in common!"

This horrified me. I just couldn't accept that this was from God. I knew from that moment on, I would spend the next several years finding out why this is so—and what can be done to solve it.

So, how has that task gone? Well, I've found out over the past year and a half. Every other week, a group of guys and I meet for lunch to talk about our faith. And we gather because we want to. Who are these guys?

They're the ones from the gym. That's right—the same guys who picked on each other's faith. Now, every month, they come to talk—and focus on C-S-G.

I want you to meet these guys. They have something important to tell us.

One-Minute Reflection:

> Do you allow doctrinal differences to dictate your attitude toward other believers?

> How would your church be different with a back-to-basics, C-S-G approach?

part three

HOW A SIMPLER FAITH SHORT-CIRCUITS

chapter 9

THE NAGGING PROBLEM OF OTHER PEOPLE'S FAITH!

I spent most of my adult years bothered by something: Whenever I saw genuine passion for God in somebody from another denomination, *I was surprised by it!*

That may sound arrogant—and, in reality, it is. But I had the typical evangelical mind-set. It says, "I'm the one with the proper essentials of the Christian faith." So I was floored by the vibrant faith of anyone operating outside my set of beliefs. How could these others, who didn't share my "correct" theology, have such an obvious connection to God?

It always caused me to marvel. If our basic views differed so much—if these other folks were "missing the mark," in Paul's words—how could they enjoy a close, rewarding relationship with the Lord?

My bafflement came from the evangelical training I received as an adult. It taught me that others didn't have the elements needed for true faith. Their beliefs were weighed down—maybe even nullified—by a lot of nonessentials and deviations from the central things. Yet the fruit of Christ was so evident, so real in these people's lives. I sensed the Spirit of Christ in them—their words, their actions, their attitudes, their interactions with others. And yet their faith seemed very different from mine in both practice and belief.

I was troubled by the conflict this caused in me. At times I had to admit that these believers' joy and faithfulness clearly surpassed mine. Could it be these people—so happy, devoted, and self-sacrificing—*did* have a personal relationship with Christ that was deeply fulfilling? If so, what did that say about my own group's theology?

Raw Desire That Connects Us to God
I couldn't help asking these questions. It was a natural reaction from what I'd been taught. Was I supposed to believe my eyes when I saw somebody outside my belief system being Christlike?

I wasn't the only one bothered by the questions these contradictions raised. At some level, these same wonderful people I encountered—all devoted followers of Jesus—most likely held a view similar to mine. Like me, they had been taught that they held the keys to faith—that they alone had the right essentials of Christianity. And when they encountered me, they must have felt as I did: "I owe it to this person to get them on the right track."

Over the years, I never let go of my nagging questions about the differences between us. It took a long time for me to come to grips with some answers. Yet what I learned had been evident to me all along, even as a child. And it's pretty simple.

When someone surrenders to the *Creator*, they're calling out to God for a *relationship*. When they want to embrace the *Savior* for the sacrifice he made, they're looking to express *gratitude*. And when they want to *be guided* by the *One* who knows what's best for them—One who actually has a design and purpose for their life—you can know such a person has grasped the three most important things in the world. God the Father, God the Son, and God the Holy Spirit.

In short, *it is a person's raw desire that connects him to the Creator-Savior-Guide.* So what if a person has denominational add-ons woven into their daily life? That doesn't preclude them from a deep and genuine connection to the Lord.

Jesus addresses this very subject.

Christ's Warnings Not to Judge by Outward Things

Jesus actually warned against judging people by their add-ons. Outward things can be deceiving—and usually are.

The clearest example of this is Christ's parable of the Good Samaritan. The Samaritans were hated and distrusted by the Jews for their distorted theology. In a Jew's eyes, the Samaritans had a whole different idea of God's plan for humankind. Yet Jesus wasn't put off by the Samaritans' religious add-ons. A responsive heart is what mattered to Jesus—not the specifics of theology. He found bad theology everywhere he went. His mission was to seek and save the lost.

But the lawmakers and Pharisees of Christ's day placed all their focus on the nonessentials. They emphasized rituals and minutiae rather than loving God and showing compassion to others. It was a way for religious leaders to feel superior—and to exclude undesirables from their group. Yet their focus on narrow, manmade things blinded them to what was really important. Jesus continually pointed that out to them.

It's this very attitude—one that's quick to dismiss another's faith, based on a standard of nonessentials—that had been passed down to me. It made me arrogant in a way I never would have thought of as offensive. In fact, I thought I was being righteous.

A Move to Repentance

As I look back, I'm heartsick that I ever viewed anyone with such skepticism. I've spent years repenting of it. And I've had to ask myself, "How did I ever come to such a place?"

I can only answer with my own story. As I've told it over the years, I have discovered it's very similar to a multitude of others'—including probably yours.

One-Minute Reflection:

> How often have you been floored by the vibrant faith of someone whose beliefs were different from yours?
>
> Is your connection to God found in a raw desire for him—or in something else?

chapter 10

CATHOLIC BOY—IN PARADISE?

When my flight first touched down in San Diego, I thought I'd landed in paradise.

For two years I had played football at a small college on Staten Island. Now I was about to fulfill a dream: to play Division I NCAA football. I was somewhat undersized for a lineman, but I'll forever be grateful to the coaches at San Diego State for taking a chance on me as a walk-on player.

Southern California was a world away—literally—from the one I knew back on the east coast. Not only was the landscape different but so were the people—the attitudes, the dress, the approaches to life. Everything was laid-back and everyone was mellow. In some ways it was refreshing. But I also desired a deeper connection. Having a Christian faith, I was eager to meet others who had a belief in God.

The first Christians I encountered at college were involved with a well-known campus ministry. I had never heard of this group—though I would soon learn their reach extended throughout the world. I was immediately taken by their passion.

These were kids like me who had a personal relationship with God. With faith of my own, I was glad to find them.

Discovering Evangelicals

My new brothers and sisters called themselves evangelicals. And they were able to articulate things about faith I had always sensed but never had words to express. They framed belief in terms that suddenly made sense to me. They used words like "saved," "accepting Christ as Savior," and "personal relationship with the Lord." These phrases brought real meaning to concepts I'd never been able to verbalize.

I could hardly believe my luck in meeting these friends. On the outside, we had so little in common—yet in reality we had *everything* in common! We shared the most important thing in the world. And that made us alike in the most important ways.

I was thrilled with the "different-ness" they brought to my life. These new faith-friends weren't afraid to make their joy known. They even offered it to strangers. That's what the gospel was meant for, I thought. Theirs was a bold, take-no-prisoners approach to faith—and it appealed to me. In fact, they challenged me about my own pursuit of Christ.

Puzzled by a Mentor's Questions

To help new believers mature in their faith, this group assigned to all newcomers a mentor—either a student who'd been around for a few years, or a college graduate who lived near the campus.

I was paired with a guy who was very encouraging. Yet, as I opened up to him, something made me feel unsettled. Whenever I spoke of my spiritual background—which, of course, was entirely Catholic—he cast doubt on my faith experience.

That puzzled me. I felt I'd understood everything he and the group were talking about: knowing Christ as my Savior, experiencing a personal relationship with him, following him with my whole heart. Now my mentor was telling me these things weren't part of the "Catholic experience"—therefore, how could I have ever been a Christian? According to him, I wasn't saved until I made Christ my Savior by a conscious decision—and by conscious action. I needed to say the sinner's prayer to receive him into my heart.

This was news to me. I *believed*—and everything I knew from my own religious background assured me I was a Christian. So I didn't necessarily absorb my mentor's doubts about my faith. Nor anyone else's, whenever my faith was challenged by a peer. I didn't really question my own faith experience.

But at that stage of my life, I didn't have the knowledge or confidence to rebut their assertions. I couldn't explain to my new friends the deep faith that had stirred in me throughout the years I'd attended mass with my mother. It was the same passion I heard them describing in their walk with Christ—the same passion that moved them to share God's plan with utter strangers. In fact, I had recognized it in them because I knew it for myself!

Whenever the subject of faith origins came up, I learned to clam up. Deep down, I always wanted to reveal more—but I sensed it would only be met with skepticism.

Focusing on the Margins
The college years are a crucial time in the formation of any person's identity. I longed for these new friends to acknowledge my faith journey to that point in my life—and maybe even be excited for me. To me, this wasn't the beginning of something—it was the exciting next step.

To them, it seemed otherwise. It hurt me that they were critiquing my faith journey, almost grading it. They chose to focus on the folly of my church's marginal beliefs rather than the power of the substance at the center—the cross of Jesus Christ.

The truth is, there was enough folly in both my old church and this new group to fertilize a cornfield. All groups have a degree of folly, whether or not they want to acknowledge it.

I considered these new people friends. So why didn't they accept my passion for the Father, Son, and Holy Ghost—the Creator, Savior, and Guide? My faith—my life—centered on the Triune God even then. We had that decidedly in common. Why not enrich that centrality, instead of tossing it out with skepticism?

Instead, their approach was to "detox" me from the old way and initiate me into the new. It turned out to be a time of deep sadness and confusion for me.

Confronted with a Sad Decision

Eventually, I had to make a choice: "I'm uncomfortable with some of this. But so much of it is appealing. It speaks to areas of my heart I've longed to address ever since I was a kid. I'm confused. Should I go where these people are inviting me to go? Or should I walk away—and risk staying in the same place spiritually?"

Sound familiar to you? It's a decision countless people of faith have had to decide at some point: "Do I go with this group? They seem to have my best interest at heart. But something tells me I can't agree with everything they believe or practice. If I go with them, I may have to leave some things behind that are important to me. But I don't want to stagnate. At least with these believers there's the promise of growth in Christ."

That was my thinking as I threw in my lot with the campus group. It meant leaving a precious part of my faith experience at the door: my Catholic background and all it had given me. And, in retrospect, it was a huge part of my journey of faith.

Yet that wasn't the end of the changes required. It also meant I had to adopt a new set of practices, if I was to be endeared to the group. I'm guessing maybe you can relate.

One-Minute Reflection:

When have you questioned another's faith experience out of your own ignorance?

Have you ever been forced into a compromising decision with a faith group—whether to stay or go?

chapter 11

A NEW SET OF RULES

Once I decided to join the campus group, their attitude was, "Finally! Now you're *home*."

I knew they meant well. But what they were actually saying was, "Now your faith is *legitimate*. You have an approved version of Christianity. This is what a believer's life should look like, sound like, and be like."

Not long after joining, the group started to inform me of all the things I had wrongly believed. I was astonished. I was equally amazed by the number of things I was told I had to believe to be part of the group. These were things I'd never heard—they were new to me as a Christian. Confession and baptism took on different dimensions, subtle but significant. Taking communion had a different feel to it—again a subtle difference, but a significant one, not just in practice but in its very meaning.

Adopting "Spiritual Practices" Particular to the Group
There were also new spiritual practices I had to observe. I saw

pretty clearly that these were associated with the organization. (They had never been part of my Catholic faith.) And they were presented to me as being the mark of genuine Christianity.

I probably don't have to tell you: These "practices" became expectations. And the expectations became standards. And the standards became a quick, easy means of judging somebody's "level of spirituality."

After a while, I felt as if my faith had been reconstituted completely. It was as if I had taken a piece of clothing to the cleaners, and when I went to pick it up it was an entirely new suit. It was a wholesale spiritual change.

I want to acknowledge that, at the time, the change felt good to me. I probably needed just that kind of jumpstart. It showed me how to pursue a deeper, more meaningful relationship with the Lord. And the things I learned during that period as a neophyte evangelical would prove deeply important to me over the years in my faith story. It was my introduction to a segment of the church I would call home for the next twenty-five years.

For the moment, I had changed denominations. I was on my way in life—supplied with the equipping of a new Christian group.

Unable to Shake a Nagging Feeling
But during that evangelical experience in college, I always felt something was amiss.

I still wondered why my fellow believers couldn't accept how I had come to know God. The denomination of my youth had not only introduced me to Jesus—they had nurtured my passion for him. *It was the very reason why I was there among these new friends.* Yet my new group was convinced the Catholic Church had totally missed the boat on issues central to true faith.

Nobody in the group ever asked me anything about my story. Whenever I referred to my Catholic background, it was immediately dismissed or ignored. It was as if it'd had no spiritual meaning whatsoever—or had never happened. The fact is, I had a deeply passionate relationship with Jesus before I'd ever met anybody in this group—but that was irrelevant to everyone.

In retrospect, I probably wasn't alone. There were probably other kids there from mainline church backgrounds—kids who had been drawn by the same appealing things I saw. I wonder now if they learned to keep quiet about their faith background, as I did. (And if, in turn, they'd learned to keep quiet about other important things throughout their life, in order to fit in. Especially in their church.)

Any talk about what constituted a spiritual life was a set agenda with this group. Few things were open for discussion. If you followed the prescribed guidelines, your spiritual life would look a certain way. And the presumption was this way was pleasing to God. Any other way was off base.

Going Home in a New Suit of Clothes
Like a lot of young people, this all rubbed off on me to the point that it annoyed my friends and family. I went back to New Jersey wearing that brand-new suit of faith. You can probably imagine the scenario. I showed up excited to talk about what I thought was "the right way."

Needless to say, I was met with some skepticism. Especially by my father, brother, and uncles. Most of them graciously shrugged me off. But their puzzled looks told me everything I needed to know. Their unstated reaction was: "I knew you as religious before. But this stuff you're talking about now—it's supposed to be something better?" They must have thought, "Eddie, give us a chance to think about what you're saying here. You're coming from a different place now."

Their puzzlement at my new form of faith didn't really affect me. It didn't make me question my newly adopted views on communion, baptism, and the like. But looking back, I see more clearly what was happening. It was my first experience in *passing on the curse of denominationalism*.

I had absorbed an attitude—one that caused me to look at someone else with skepticism. To question their faith experience. To erect a subtle but definite barrier between us.

I'm still having to shake off the vestiges of that attitude.

A Sea of Broken Spirits

That attitude of "spiritual superiority" was something I learned. I got it from the campus ministry.

I might be tempted to say this attitude is the spirit driving a lot of campus ministries. Young adults are simply more emotional and idealistic in their approach to life. Why should their approach to *spiritual life* be any different?

But I can't lay it all at the feet of youthful idealism. The fact is, I've served in churches over the past three decades that are just as rigid in their practices. And just as unrelenting in their nonessential beliefs.

The results of that rigidity in the lives of well-meaning Christians thirty years down the road aren't pretty. It has ended up in a lot of broken spirits.

And a lot of drifting, disconnected men.

One-Minute Reflection:

Was there a period in your life when you passed down "the curse of denominationalism"?

When did you give up your efforts to preach to others "the right way"? What caused you to give it up?

chapter 12

SIX MEN—AND A BOY

Fast-forward twenty-five years...

Every time I enter the restaurant door I head straight for the back. That's where our regular table is.

Usually when I take my seat, somebody is taking a ribbing over his team's loss that week. Or, all faces may be turned to one guy, who's facing some crisis, major or minor. Maybe a family member's in trouble. Or there's a conflict on his job.

Within minutes, we're all up to speed on each other. We get what's going on that week in each other's lives. And we're happy to lend an ear. Maybe offer support in some way, if we can. Mostly, we're just grateful to know. We realize it could be our turn in the hot seat the following week.

Each of the men in our group is more or less in middle age. And the issues of life for men at this stage don't stop coming. You're looking at aging parents, maturing kids, financial strains going in both directions. The men who gather around this lunch table know that God has given us each other. And we're happy for it. We come here faithfully—because we *want* to be here.

Our time at this table sometimes makes me reflect on my fifteen years in men's ministry. I always served in that role as a lay minister. I never pursued it as a full-time position or took a salary for it. I was simply glad to do it. It's my passion. I wanted to be able to speak to men—to reach out to them and find them wherever they were: in the pews, in the gym, outside a restaurant taking a smoke.

Now, as I sit at this table and take in the faces around it, I see that but for a hair's breadth of God's grace, none of these guys might be here. *I* might not be here. I might have drifted. And for a while I did drift, in my heart.

Emerging from a Cycle of Brokenness

The funny thing is, some of these guys have been rigid themselves. Just as I learned to be. (No doubt, some of us still struggle with it!) The difference now is, they've been through their own cycles of brokenness. Judging by their grace-filled lives, you'd never guess any of them were ever rigid in any way. But the truth is, we're all susceptible—and we're all culpable.

I've learned not to blame rank-and-file believers for "the denominational curse." Anyone's rigidity is just the product of a bigger system—one that pollutes their perspective, as it did mine. After all, the only tools we believers have to work with are what our denomination has provided us.

Now, as I look at these guys, I see the faces of men who've traveled the same weary journey I have. They once were lost by denominationalism—but now are found by God. And by each other.

Calling on a Much-Needed Ear

"Guys, I need your ear on this," I tell the group. In truth, I have never needed it more.

I remind them about my son, who's away at college. He has

struggled in his faith these past few years. His questions are the normal ones that any developing young mind has at that stage of life. To those who know him, his faith remains genuine. Even his questions come from a real place—with real concerns and a deep desire to understand what doesn't seem to make sense to him.

A while back, my son made a decision on his own to become involved with a faith group on his college campus. He felt this group most closely represents Christianity as he understands it. It was similar to the flavor he grew up with.

Still, doing this was a big leap for him, because he's naturally quiet and introspective. The group is evangelical, and he decided he would feel most at home with others of that faith expression.

I gulped—hard—before relating the next part to my friends.

"It turns out this group is very conservative on a lot of things. And there are 'spiritual expectations.' These are causing him a lot of pressure. He's been told that God could—and should—reveal himself to him daily. He's supposed to 'feel the Spirit' regularly. In fact, spiritual highs are an indication of where you are with God.

"He hears a phrase used all the time by others: 'God is speaking to me.' It confuses him, because he admits he doesn't hear a clear voice or message from God. And he wishes he did."

All around the table, my friends nodded knowingly.

Stirring up Memories

As I spoke, a memory was stirred in me.

I recalled my own confusion and disappointment toward the end of my college experience. For a short while, I had accompanied a Pentecostal friend to services at his church. At one point, he and the pastor encouraged me to seek "the baptism of the Holy Spirit." They told me that whenever this happens in someone, the evidence is speaking in tongues. They said this baptism was a gift given freely by God to all believers who follow Christ sincerely.

I didn't see any reason not to seek the gift. I thought it might be another special leg in the journey of faith God meant for me. So I said yes.

With that, the pastor leaned forward and anointed my forehead with oil. Then he and my friend began praying for me there in the church office. They were waiting for a supernatural language to come forth from me.

After a half hour, I realized it just wasn't going to happen. So I stopped the pastor and my friend. I thanked them for their efforts—I knew they had meant well. Then my friend and I walked out of the church in an awkward silence.

As we got into the car, I thought to myself, *I guess it's just not meant for me*. But I had a deep, gnawing sense I had let God down.

Could it be my son was feeling the same way now?

Repeating the "Expectation" Cycle

"Guys," I told my men's group, "you all know how this goes. And you know my son. He's confused and feeling pressure. He's in need of your prayers. And, more than anything, he needs to know he's okay with *a simple faith*."

I could hardly believe the story I had just shared. *It had come full circle*. My son was experiencing the exact same thing I had thirty years before. In all that time, nothing had changed!

I looked around at each guy. I saw faces of men who had been down a long, hard road. They had won some battles and lost some—but they kept their faith. Now they only wanted a simple faith for themselves. And they were determined to have it. They were glad to come to this table and sit with each other at the foot of the cross—knowing that was enough.

I had never imagined my son would go through what I did. I

never want *any child* to have to endure those kinds of pressures. *Ever.* God never meant for our children to suffer these things in order to know him. He has something so much more beautiful in store for all of us. He designed us for a relationship of continual grace, love, blessing, and support. The kind of relationship we as parents strive to give our own children.

I wonder: When will one generation stand up to stop this madness? Who will give themselves to stop the grinding wheels of this awful machinery? Who will raise their voice for the absolute necessity of a simple faith?

Or will yet another generation be lost to a lifetime of spiritual suffering? Is another generation doomed to a hardscrabble journey like ours—one that derails them from the deep experience of love God desires for all?

Our children need us to do this. For them. *Now.*

One-Minute Reflection:

> How do you see the curse of denominationalism being passed down to the young people in your life?
>
> Are you in a group where the "spiritual expectations" are impossibly high?

part four

THE URGENT NEED FOR A SIMPLER FAITH

chapter 13

HITTING THE ADOLESCENT CEILING

Like any parent, I want my son to be able to mature and develop in his faith. At the same time, I want to spare him any unnecessary pain. And a lot of pain is caused by manmade religious practices. I'm talking about those things that chip away at our souls rather than build us up.

My son needs and wants—in short—*a simpler faith*. I want that for him, too. But I've had to conclude that the trial he's going through—one that many of us have faced—is a necessary part of growing into Christian maturity.

Think about Jesus' life. He spent a lot of his time on earth facing down the manmade practices of a self-righteous system. In every case, Jesus always brought it back to a simpler faith. His approach tells us something important—something *crucial*—about how we're to do this thing called church.

Raw Desire—and Christ's Blessing

Time after time, Christ lauded raw desire for the Father. I think of the woman with the issue of blood (Luke 8:43). Desperate to be healed, she touched the hem of Christ's garment. By law, she shouldn't have even been near him. Her mark of "uncleanness" (a spiritual law related to hygiene practices) prohibited it.

But in desperation, the woman reached out and touched Jesus. And he chose to heal her, honoring her faith.

I think of the widow who gave her last coin as an offering (Luke 21:1-4). Today, we might call this little old lady's action quaint, or even cute. After all, how far can a single coin go? But Jesus lauded her faith. He said it was the kind of belief that moves the forces of heaven.

I think of the woman at the well (John 4:1-26). Here's someone who, by "church rules," Jesus shouldn't even have been talking to. Yet he honored her questions because he saw in them the genuine seeds of faith.

I think of the Gentile official who sought out Jesus to heal his dying servant (Matthew 8:5-13). This man wasn't even in the religious fold—far from it. Yet he knew something important about Jesus. He said if Christ just gave the word, he knew his servant would be healed.

Jesus gladly honored this man's request. Yet it was much more than that. What he did amounted to answering the prayer of a person we would consider a "nonbeliever." But a believer this man was—so much so that Jesus was amazed and delighted by his raw, simple faith.

Raw Desire—Mixed with Faith

None of these people had anything to offer the Lord—anything, that is, but *their own raw need*.

And something else: their faith. They all desired God in the most basic sense. They also believed in him. They were, in a sense, kneeling at the foot of the cross. Each of them was acknowledging their need—and the only One who could meet that need.

How did Jesus respond to such people? He refused to turn them away. He honored these broken people's desire to see the Father move in their lives. According to him, they were demonstrating the greatest faith of all—and he blessed them for it.

Note that in each case, Jesus was cutting against the religious grain. He wasn't just challenging the established religious structure. He was calling for a new one. He was saying there was a new way—*a simpler way*. One that had to do with *simple desire for God*.

There were no hoops for these people to jump through. There were no leaders to please, no rituals to observe. (If anything, rituals were bypassed.)

It's a way we need to return to. And our children need it, too. We all need *the simpler way of Christ*.

Raw Desire—in a Church Environment

Three decades is a long time to live in a self-righteous religious environment. That's basically the time that elapsed between my faith experience at college and my life today as a late-forty-something Christian.

So, what happens to our faith during that time? How does it get shaped in the decades following college? What feeds our raw desire for God during our adult years in church? What's the church's plan for a Christian as he or she navigates adulthood?

In terms of the life and growth of every Christian, the church functions in three basic ways:

Church life ought to strengthen and reinforce our *belief in God*. The things we learn from the pulpit, from classes, and from each other are meant to build our faith. That doesn't happen from daily "mountaintop" experiences (though something like that can be powerful and instructive). It's meant to happen over time—as Isaiah said, "line upon line, precept upon precept."

Meanwhile, church should be *shaping our lives*. That means

leading us deeper into the character of Christ. Church should challenge us beyond the "bold convictions" of our youth, to gain wisdom for the "long haul" of life. Some aspects of life are complex by design. The point is, throughout the whole process— through all of life's up and downs—the character of Christ is being built into us.

Finally, we're given *service opportunities*. We're to demonstrate what we know of God and his nature by helping others. We learn to do his works sacrificially. And we learn to do it faithfully, over a lifetime.

The Slow Creep of Denominationalism

So you've settled into your pew for the next thirty years. You're looking forward to strengthening your belief in God . . . to seeing Christ's character built into you...to having opportunities to serve...to bless in ways you've been blessed.

We need to ask ourselves: Where, and how, does *the curse of denominational thinking* creep into this experience?

Let's face it. We all bring our judgmental baggage into our adult church experience. And there's already a denominational bias in place in whichever church we land. How does this mixture shape our belief system? Especially over thirty years?

Let me put it this way:

> If there's a constant mentality of "getting it right," how does that influence what we deem is important to God?

> If there's a constant undercurrent of, "We're right, they're wrong," how does that dictate how we serve (or don't serve) our community?

All of these subtle shadings occur in churches, to some degree. And we absorb them, whether consciously or

subconsciously. After all, church is the one physical environment where our spiritual values are forged as a community.

So it's crucial to look at how these things affect us over time. I've already mentioned one effect of this kind of environment: *You absorb the curse of denominational thinking.* Of course, I'm using the word "denomination" loosely. You may belong to a *non*denominational church—but it's still part of a bigger "faith group" or network. How does this thinking show up? You start to view those outside your group with suspicion. For example, many Newbies may proudly have no "denomination." But they do have a mentality of, "We're right, you're wrong."

This mixture—of existing church biases, plus youthful, zealous biases—can't help affecting how we do church. And how we view others, Christian or not.

Hitting the Adolescent Ceiling

Something happens in the lives of many vibrant young churches. They run smack into something that researchers call "the adolescent ceiling."

See, evangelical churches are great at providing answers to concrete questions about life. They give us reliable thoughts about meaning, purpose, belief. These are the kinds of things that fuel zealous young believers.

So, by and large, we're great at creating rah-rah excitement—whether about evangelism, or bomb-proof theologies, or even pet political issues. In this way, churches are sort of an extension of campus ministries. The point is to get the troops motivated and send them out, with all their inexhaustible energy, to change the world with their message.

But what happens beyond this initial "excitement" phase? In this area, evangelical churches don't do so well. We aren't so great when it comes to building into believers a "mature faith." By this I mean a faith that deepens over time—through life experience, through ups and downs, through joys and obstacles. Growing into this kind of mature faith is the subject of most of the New Testament epistles.

Let me give an example of where a lot of churches fail at this: *They avoid addressing life's more complex issues.* Take politics, for example. All of us are influenced by what we hear from the pulpit and by what we hear throughout our spiritual community. This includes political convictions. In many churches—evangelical or mainline, Newbie or Old Guard—there's only one way to think politically. Suddenly, someone with a differing opinion isn't just different. He or she is *morally suspect*. And that casts doubt on the authenticity of their faith.

In my experience, this is one area where a lot of men go off the rails and eventually consider leaving. They can't buy into the "group think" their church mandates. I saw this happen with countless numbers of guys. There would be an oversimplification of an ambiguous issue. Say, the pastor reframes a political issue into a spiritual one. And there's no freedom to question or discuss it.

Thus a "code of silence" is enforced. And it drives guys in one of two directions: either *passive compliance* or *active retreat*.

It's an adolescent approach. And when churches tout it—"Everything is black and white, with clear answers"—it leads to a whole lot of manmade junk. The kind of garbage that gets in the way of a mature faith, a faith that's willing to view life in all its complexities.

But that's only one way our raw desire for God gets derailed.

One-Minute Reflection:

> Do you know a "nonbeliever" who shows a "raw desire" for God?

> Does your church turn an ambiguous issue into something cut-and-dried, black-and-white, with a "clear spiritual" answer? How do you react when that happens?

chapter 14

GREAT STARTS AND REAL MOMENTS

As a couple, our story is like many other evangelicals'. Lynette and I both came from non-evangelical backgrounds—for me Catholic, for her Lutheran. Evangelical faith made a big difference for both of us. Before we met, we each took a serious step forward when we encountered evangelicalism. It caused us to be more intentional about our relationship with God. And we both got a crash course in cross-denominational training.

When we married, Lynette and I both wanted a solid faith experience for our children. As we looked for a church, we learned the "big box" churches thriving in suburbia were mostly evangelical. They had become a huge gathering place for Catholics and mainline Protestants like us—people who had felt a bit disenfranchised in their old group.

Lynette and I both reveled in the upbeat nature and worship of these suburban churches. Dynamic worship and powerfully gifted teaching swept us into the fold. It didn't take long for us to land in one where we felt like we were "home."

As we settled into that first church, we brought our

experiences with all the good and the bad. And to be perfectly honest, there was much more good than bad. There were wonderful programs for young families like ours. There were also programs that reached out to the community. I believe the acts of service I saw happening there would have made God proud of His people. I eagerly got involved with them.

Something else good happened for Lynette and me at that stage. God became more personal to us. We both had loved the Lord growing up in our denominations. But in those churches, God was spoken of as an abstraction rather than a person. Now, in this new evangelical expression, we *felt* God's nearness more than before. We believed He was personally involved with us. And, as most evangelicals will tell you, there's no greater feeling in the world.

Our church was like any other. I've already mentioned some ways we hit the infamous adolescent ceiling. It began with the usual stuff: an imbalanced focus on evangelism commitments …a pressure to conform without questioning…an encouraged dependence on the pastor's eloquent sermons.

To be sure, Lynette and I had a great start there. Those early years made a tremendous difference in our lives. But as time progressed, we had more and more tangles with manmade structures—and I had less and less meaningful growth in my love for God.

My Burden for "Everyguy"

I mentioned upfront in this book that my alter ego is Joe Palooka. I have a heart for the everyday Christian who's doing his or her best to follow Christ from Sunday to Sunday. The fact is, most of us are unbelievably harried by the normal demands of life—making a living, raising kids, providing the best we know how. Through it all, we try to lead a life of faith that pleases God.

As a harried young husband myself back then, I had a

growing passion toward others who strove to love God. Seeing their desire moved me more than anything. It's what eventually led me to direct the men's ministry in our big-box church.

You can imagine my excitement when I saw the Christian men's movement emerging in the 1990s. Here was something that would help young families, while feeding and building up Christian men in their desire for God. Little did I know, this movement—originally meant for our benefit—would be the undoing of a lot of men!

A Day in the Life of a "Men's Movement" Man
As the movement grew, suddenly men were in the church's crosshairs. Books were published, ministries popped up, experts were touted. Everybody was intent on teaching us men how to be "spiritual leaders" in our home.

Needless to say, the expectations put on men were high. One popular bumper sticker read, "Real Men Pray." Another in vogue was, "A Man's Man Is a Godly Man."

It was all supposedly about showing men their spiritual position and purpose. In my opinion, it ended up overwhelming most of us. I did everything that was prescribed. But instead of building up my "spiritual authority," I felt like a spiritual failure at times.

To be a godly dad, I got up every day making sure I wore a diaper bag over my shoulder. I ended up being like Michael Keaton's character in *Mr. Mom*. True victory meant being adequately prepared with Pampers the next time a poop arrived—and they came with great frequency in those years.

I tried to have meaningful prayer times with my wife. I did my best to decipher her "love language." I tried reading the Bible to my kids and praying with them after dinner each night. All this took place after a full day of hustling as a sales rep, with much of my time spent on the road.

Meanwhile, I had to stay on track with my own spiritual growth. So I got involved in a men's Bible study. Lynette and I also joined a couples' Bible study, to make sure we were involved in spiritual community. I kept up my roles in our church's outreach and service ministries, so I wouldn't wither in that area. In short, I was doing it all.

Yet I was so busy trying to be "all things to all people" that eventually I got resentful and fed up.

In the end, the Christian men's movement created a lot of pressure for men to get everything right. In hindsight, maybe the leaders made it more complicated than it needed to be. In that sense, it mirrored the failed "supermom" expectations that saddled women in the 1980s.

Don't get me wrong. The Christian men's movement did succeed in getting men excited about their faith. But the dump truck full of expectations—to be Super Dad, Super Husband, Super Spiritual Leader, Super Christian Man—ended up squelching most of the excitement. Who could do it all?

A Need to Be Real

A popular book came in the wake of that movement: John Eldredge's *Wild at Heart*. Eldredge wrote eloquently about what a man longs for in his soul: an adventure to pursue, a battle to fight, and a beauty to rescue. Tell me, would that not appeal to guys? It all sounded exciting, edgy, very guy-oriented. It certainly had my attention.

What really rang a bell with me was something else John said about guys. He wrote, "Christianity, as it currently exists, has done some terrible things to men."

I blew a sigh of relief over this. The way Eldredge wrote about manhood, it sounded real—not hyper-spiritual. The things he talked about were earthy, grounded. And his message appealed to women, too, when they saw what kind of man John was talking about becoming.

Honestly, I don't know what the right balance is for men. But something in John's writing spoke deeply to me. And it had the needed effect when I started leading our church's men's ministry.

Finding the Key

The guys who came to our first men's meetings sincerely wanted to grow in godliness. They just didn't know where to start.

So at first we kept it simple. We set up events so men could just get to know each other. Soon our numbers were growing with every event we held—and that was exciting to see. But after a while, I realized we were still only "a mile wide and an inch deep."

If we were going to actually minister to men—if we wanted to be more than just another rah-rah men's thing—I knew we had to get real.

Our church had been holding an annual retreat for men. That year, the number of guys who signed up was off the charts. So I decided to use the opportunity to make an important point. I made sure to secure one of the speaking slots during the retreat. My plan might have been risky—but, win or lose, I was going to be real.

"Guys," I said into the mic when my turn came, "I need to be straight with you about something. I've been traveling more in my work recently. And I've been battling with the TV in my hotel room. I'm not always winning that battle."

Silence. Every one of those guys could identify with me.

"You know what I'm talking about. It's tough when you're on the road and alone. I need to take steps to give myself the best chance of success in that fight.

"The truth is, we're all subject to that fight. Why? Because we're bad guys? No. Because one thing is true for every man in this room. We all have *'the curse of the 'nads.'*"

Thankfully, I got a laugh.

"I know this is an odd thing to be throwing out to you here. But I don't want to hide it from you. I'm not going to pretend the problem doesn't exist in my life. I can't do that and keep standing in front of you. If we can't be real with each other—real before God, *here*, in this place—there's no place we can."

There were a lot of guys in that room. And you could feel the relief, the freedom in the air. Any trace of pretense went out the window. In an instant, these guys knew they could be fully themselves. Nothing more was said along the lines of what I'd shared. But the level of candor and openness changed the atmosphere for the entire weekend. Later, more than half of those guys contacted me to thank me.

It was a huge experience for us. Everything had turned for us in that moment. I'm not saying our men's group became super-spiritual giants—we didn't. But what we did become was *real*. In the weeks and months that followed, grace abounded. Guys flourished. You could see the weight lifting from the guys' shoulders. They came alive. Chains of silence were being broken.

It taught me something. I grew convinced this kind of candor has to be present—*everywhere*. A church can't set some high spiritual bar and hope men clear it. You simply can't have pretense of any kind. *You cannot hide real-life crap!* Men won't buy into it. And besides, inner realities have a way of eventually becoming outer ones. That's just the way we're made.

After everything—the energy of the men's movement, my own efforts to be Mr. Mom, my desire to be Mr. Spiritual Leader—it all boiled down to one thing: *being real*. It's what made me a man—and a man of God.

If we want to keep it simple, we've got to keep it real. It's the only way.

When we don't, it all begins to unravel. Our church would eventually find that out the hard way.

One-Minute Reflection:

> You read about my experience with the men's movement. Have you ever felt overwhelmed by those kinds of "spiritual expectations"?
>
> How does it feel to think of sexual struggles as something normal instead of as a "spiritual failure"?

chapter 15

MEN—IN A SPIRITUAL SOUP LINE

When I started leading the men's ministry, I saw a lot of hunger in those guys. I felt my job was to nurture that hunger to good fruit. And we did see a lot of good fruit in our group.

Yet over time, the hunger I saw in them slowly dissipated. More and more of the guys grew disconnected from the church. I began taking each of them aside to ask about it. To a man, they all said they felt like they weren't fitting in.

Was it the group, I asked? Had somebody done something to alienate them? Or had I? No, they assured me.

For some guys, the problem was the "group think" mind-set of the congregation. Other guys were troubled that the congregation practically hero-worshipped the pastor. The greatest number of disaffected guys told me they couldn't be open with anyone in the church—about their disagreements with doctrine, their faith questions, their struggles with sin.

This last issue was a big one. The bar of "spiritual victory" was set incredibly high by the leaders. It created a stifling atmosphere—just the opposite of the openness and freedom that we all had experienced at the retreat. At church, it seemed more important for leaders to look like they had it together. That discouraged regular guys from being open about their struggles. And it fostered an atmosphere of pretense.

No matter who you are, you can only suppress things for so long. I've said it before in a previous chapter: *God can only deal with our reality.* The only place his grace can be applied is a place of honesty. But how can anybody be honest if the expectation is perfection?

The Next Impossible Measurement: Performance!
Ministers, are you getting this? Tell me, do you know men who don't come to church with their wives or families anymore? Well, I know those men. And I know the reasons most of them don't show up anymore. They've explained it to me.

It's not that they've turned their backs on God. *It's that the church has turned its back on them.* We haven't offered these men a safe place to be open—about themselves or their struggles.

I'm not just talking about the local church. I'm talking about the entire Christian "industry"—the books, recordings, and videos that are produced. Only a small percentage of these things speak about maturity in faith—or with any brutal honesty about our sin nature. Much of what's being churned out is on church growth, having success in life, having the right theology. That does nothing for the church's main mission. It only serves the status quo.

Worse, these products create standards for a "performance" that no Christian—man or woman—can meet. And that creates undue burdens.

Even if a guy does his best to meet these impossible standards—and I tried as hard as the next guy—he'll eventually break down. Human perfection was God's design, but the Fall changed all that. Now, no one can achieve it.

The whole system is a setup for failure. Yet we keep insisting on it. Why? It's much easier to measure an outward "performance"—as a Christian husband, father, leader—than to measure genuine maturity in Christ.

A Soul-Deadening Choice: Jump in, or Jump out
I had a unique vantage point on all this as a men's ministry leader. And I can tell you on good authority: These manmade expectations are the reasons why men are gone. It isn't because they've gone off the deep end into sin. And it isn't because they don't want God.

It's because deep down they don't believe they're serving Christ by agreeing with some politicized agenda . . . or hero-worshipping the pastor . . . or emphasizing some manmade add-on . . . or meeting some standard dreamed up by a perfectionist jerk in his ivory tower.

God made men for something different from all these manmade hoops. And yet they aren't often given the opportunity to do the things God designed them for. Occasionally, they're asked to serve in a meaningful way—say, once a year, on a short-term mission. But more often, the opportunities they're presented with are meant to sustain the church itself in some way. I'm all for that—but not when the aim is to keep the machinery going, rather than to be Christ to each other and to the community.

It all becomes meaningless after a while. And over time, it batters men's souls. Rather than fight city hall, they just leave. Or, if they stay, they forfeit a part of their soul. Some decide to jump into the system's machinery. At least that way they can get strokes for their "performance."

I don't say this with any personal embitterment. The fact is, any man can "thrive" in this kind of environment—if he chooses to make the compromise. But it's a deadly bargain. This kind of "thriving" doesn't build up anybody's soul—because it isn't God's design. Instead, you end up replacing true spiritual hunger with a performance that drives you further away from it—and away from a life of grace.

Dreams from Their Youth

There's something tragic in all this. See, these men were tapped by God in their youth, or maybe even midlife. His Spirit stirred them and drew them to the Savior. And He placed inside them His own passion to see a broken world redeemed. He put in them a desire to bear witness to the world about His bottomless grace, mercy, and love.

So, back to my original question: What does thirty years in a judgmental environment do?

I've found out through my current guys' group. By listening to their stories.

When we get together for Bible study every two weeks, I hear stories that are a lot like mine. These men have been through the ringer and come out on the other side. Somehow their faith survived the "denominational" meat grinder. Now they're finding what they need in a simpler way of faith—one that's stripped of all the crap.

Their faith is being clarified month after month by . . . *freedom*. Freedom to reignite their passion for God. Freedom to get rid of the remnants of the crap that still clings to them. Freedom to be as open and honest as they need to be, knowing they'll get the support they need.

In short, I see before me a half-dozen guys being energized by a certain discipline. It's the discipline of *setting aside everything they see as manmade*. This discipline has made their focus laser-like. And it allows them to fix on simple realities: knowing their Creator, showing gratitude to their Savior, and listening to their Guide. These simple things have led them to a mature faith.

I want to put out a call to all ministers reading this. How would you like a more energized congregation? Instead of one that's drained, with one foot already out the door? You know better than anybody: God's people are energized only when they're connected to His design and purpose for them. We're supposed to be about his works—not some manmade performance standard. It's the manmade B.S. that drains us.

It's time for all of us to take action—and to do it for our sons and daughters. For our drifting, disconnected brothers and sisters. And for the sake of the church's soul.

I'm convinced—if there's a men's movement to be had, it's about following our Lord's example in this matter. It's time to move forward—to break down every barrier that a stunted, adolescent church foists on its people.

Talk about having a battle to fight.

It takes more guts than you think to have a simpler faith.

One-Minute Reflection:

Do you try to measure your "performance" as a Christian?

Name a safe place (or person) where you can be open about your struggles or sins.

part five

CHURCH BARRIERS TO A SIMPLER FAITH

chapter 16

SETTING THE TABLE—AND STACKING THE DECK

I've talked about three things that drive men away from church: Group think, pastor worship, and performance standards.

Now it's time to take a nitty-gritty look at what the church, at its worst, does best: *denominationalism*. Again, I use the word loosely. I'm talking about an affiliation we make with a faith group. Or, simply, a theological bent.

Everybody has an affiliation or a bent. It's unavoidable. But the important thing isn't that we have one. It's what we *do* with that affiliation or bent that ultimately pleases God—or irks him.

The "Blink" Moment of Doctrinal Separation

A certain scenario keeps repeating itself in my life. It's something that never ceases to frustrate me. It's this: Anytime I introduce myself to another believer, I'm always questioned: "Where are you going to church?"

It's a normal question to ask. But what they really want to know is, "What 'denomination' are you involved in? I might want to have fellowship with you, but first I need to gauge your belief system."

Our conversation might begin on common ground—say, some aspect of C-S-G, the Father, Son, and Holy Spirit. But before long, we're veering down divergent paths. And the reason is *doctrinal separation*—nothing more. In the end, we're kept from fellowship and all its glorious possibilities *by nonessentials*.

I always part ways with the other person in an air of disappointment. We never make plans to see each other again. Each time, I leave anguished, wondering, "Why can't we stay on this basic path? It would only unite us. There's so much blessing to enjoy, so much we could accomplish together—in faith, in community, in service. As it stands, we can't even talk to each other."

Can We Blame Each Other?
I've learned not to blame my fellow Christians for this. After all, we've only learned what has been taught to us by our group. I turn my disappointment instead on denominations—the source of all the add-ons, and thus the barrier-making.

I wondered what it would be like for believers to "leave everything at the door" when we start a conversation about faith. If only we could connect more deeply on the central things—specifically, C-S-G, the Triune God. What would that look like? And what would it produce?

Would our groups still be suspicious of each other? Or would we find an incredible bond through the awesome common ground we share?

Is that what *a simpler faith* would ultimately mean? A dynamic of fellowship healthier than any we've ever experienced? A strengthened hope for seeing God's work extended throughout the earth?

Where would we begin this kind of work?

As with most things, it all starts at home. I'm talking now about our "faith home"—*the local church*.

Naming the Head of the Table

Denominations are an intractable part of history. They came about mostly as church leaders separated over doctrines. And so we've inherited most of the manmade, add-on problems that plague us today.

But how does this trouble *persist* down through the generations? Why haven't we been able to shake it off? It's because denominationalism gets ingrained at a *local level*.

Think of a local church as a table where the family gathers. Every group—from families to schools to churches to businesses—assigns somebody to sit at the head of the table. And that chosen leader is put in charge of all major decisions. In churches—especially evangelical churches—this is where a lot of trouble begins.

In a typical scenario, the leader has his own agenda. He sets things into motion hoping to achieve whatever he envisions. The problem with this approach is: Who decides what is *God's agenda*? One person in charge of that decision potentially leads to all kinds of problems.

Absolute power does corrupt. It's been proven again and again—and churches are no exception. If there isn't a group to provide oversight or checks-and-balances, things can't be kept healthy. It's why some denominations require churches to do all decision-making by a board of elders. This helps a church steer clear of control issues. But even then, a board can be "stacked" or cowed by a powerful pastor.

Sometimes the people themselves give too much power to the pastor. (And they do it willingly. More on this later.) Ask yourself about that dynamic in your church. Do you sense that your congregation's survival depends on your main preacher? Buddy, you've already got a problem. It's true that every church needs just one figurehead to keep it afloat. But that person is God.

Without healthy, humble checks-and-balances, we set the

stage for abuses of power. And, of course, we usually get what we ask for.

Scandals—at Both Ends of the Table
I've been a part of several large evangelical Christian groups. In my experience, an abuse of power at the top has been more common than not. That's sad to say, I know. But it's also the experience of many reading this book.

If a leader has control issues, he may position himself as being beyond reproach. Phrases like "the Lord's anointed" or "God's chosen" get put into circulation. Pretty soon the leader is elevated to inscrutability.

We've all seen where this leads. Any middle-aged American knows about the televangelist scandals of the 1980s. We were shocked and saddened to see preachers with international reputations get caught with their hand in the cookie jar, in shameful ways.

Yet those were only the high-profile cases. The same thing happens all the time in churches of every denomination, but without the media fireworks. Oddly, our reaction in the wake of any church scandal is usually the same. We're left asking, "Why didn't anyone see this coming? How was the leader allowed to go so off course?"

But many did see it coming. The real question is: Why didn't they say something? Or, more accurately: Why weren't they *allowed* to say something? Why wasn't there a healthy forum in which to voice their concerns?

In the Jim Bakker-Jimmy Swaggart ministries, the organizational structure protected the leader. It didn't allow for anybody to challenge their word or vision. That in itself led to tragic results.

But I'll tell you what's equally tragic. *Those same firewalls prevented anybody from helping those leaders.* It kept out anyone who could have reached them with the help they needed before it was too late. Sane voices did try to confront the leaders, but those voices were silenced by the "yes men" surrounding them.

The local church and her pastor are not immune. God is no respecter of persons. We all need the same amount of grace to avoid sin and shameful scandal. And this means our pastors—no matter how powerful we want them to appear—need our help from day one.

Worshipping these guys has been one of the worst plagues the church has ever brought on itself. I want to take a closer look at where these breakdowns occur. And together we can call on God to help us patch the walls.

One-Minute Reflection:

> Are you aware of your theological bent? Do you avoid fellowshipping with other believers because of nonessentials?
>
> How is your church structured organizationally? Does it allow for healthy questioning?

chapter 17

DOIN' THE "CORPORATE CREEP"

If you work in the corporate world, you know how hard it is to make your voice heard. And if you start to raise concerns about the way things are run, getting an ear is that much harder.

It's common for business leaders to keep company issues secret from their employees. If a worker raises a serious concern, he's usually told to submit to the company's authority. If he goes public with those concerns, he's called a whistleblower, and he's ostracized by the entire organization (as well as by the public).

This kind of controlling dynamic leads to all kinds of secretive sickness. Think of the Enron scandal. Maybe you've seen the documentary, *The Smartest Guys in the Room*. That movie reveals just how corrupt smart people can become. Their greediest impulses can run rampant if there's no authoritative voice to challenge them.

Thousands of hardworking people at Enron lost everything they had worked for. And all because the guys at the top weren't kept in check. They freely took multiple millions in bonuses for themselves. Yes, the "smart guys" ended up robbing the company of everything. And they brought down the whole house around them.

I want to be fair—not all corporations or CEOs are this unhealthy. My personal experience has been positive, and there are many fine examples of well-run, even philanthropic companies that benefit their workers and communities. But there are enough headlines from Wall Street bungles alone to prove my point.

A Hard Lesson for Churches—from "the World"

Christians don't want to think this kind of thing can happen in church leadership. We're taught to give the benefit of the doubt, especially to church leaders. But you'd be surprised how often some of the same corporate dynamics are at work in houses of faith. And they can lead to the same kind of secretive sickness.

It's common for any believer to have honest questions about his or her church's practices. But in an unhealthy faith environment, those questions can be seen as challenges to authority and to the leader's vision.

Suddenly, people who raise honest questions are called "divisive." They get labeled "problem people." At their worst, church leaders make a dissenter look like an agent of the devil. Bible verses are cherry-picked to force compliance to the group and to silence all challenges.

If the concerned questioner persists, he's given an ultimatum: "It's obvious you can't let go of this pet issue of yours. If you choose to continue, you may be more comfortable worshipping elsewhere."

Sadly, some believers are shamed into leaving. And some never enter a church's doors again.

The Appeal of the Corporate Model

A corporate structure in a church allows for this kind of abusive scenario. Yet it's a structure the church has readily adopted.

It's hard to argue with a business model that's brought prosperity to so many people. The corporate model has been around for over a century and companies have learned to refine their operations, becoming highly efficient systems for delivering products or services in profitable ways.

Because it's been successful for so long, the corporate model is deeply ingrained in our culture. It's no surprise it would eventually seep into the church. Sometime around the 1980s, denominations began flocking to the corporate system. They pushed their pastors to apply corporate practices so their churches would run efficiently. (Before that, most churches relied on models that had been used for over a century.)

The rest is literally history. The past three decades have become known as the era of the "church-growth movement." Some people think the movement is on its last legs. (That's especially true of younger Christians, who reject the idea of huge, impersonal megachurches.) But back then, the wisdom was: If you want a successful church, you must have continual growth. And to sustain that growth, you have to apply corporate principles.

Here's the question that was never really asked: *What does growth look like to God? And does the corporate model foster it?*

How a Church Implements the Corporate Model

It all begins with the staff. The corporate staff system is designed to keep the ship moving forward.

The staff is usually headed by a senior leader who assembles a team. Other models govern through an elder/deacon structure, but even then the dominant figure is usually the lead pastor. Believe me, in a world where the sermon is the center of everything—and one guy's preaching is the main draw on Sunday mornings—that's where the power resides.

It doesn't matter how evenly you distribute power at the top. The Sunday preaching pastor becomes the default leader. All real influence rests with him. He may try to dismiss that power all he wants. But if the people have assigned it to him, he's got it, whether anyone likes it or not. He's the CEO, by default or design.

If you've ever worked for a large company, you know how hard it is to get into the CEO's office. The same is true in a corporate-run church. The senior pastor isn't just walled off—he takes on messiah-like status. You get the feeling you should just nod and agree in his presence, rather than be open and honest. But even if he downplays his status, it's reinforced by the leadership team and staff. And sometimes even by the congregation—because they *want* a pastor with messiah-like status.

This corporate-like structure allows for a shroud of secrecy over how things are run. It opens the door to hiding spots for its leaders. And that's exactly where the model breaks down in a church: *Doing church should be all about transparency.* Leadership needs to happen in front of people—not behind a drape.

Entangled in the Drive for Success
The corporate model also leads to a "success" mind-set in a church. And, naturally, it starts to reflect the world's standard of success, not Christ's.

I have a close friend who is the senior pastor of a church. Before that, he served as executive pastor at another church. (The position of "executive pastor" itself came about because of the corporate model. When churches started emphasizing "growth," they required a lot more administration than a preacher could provide.) Essentially, the role of the executive pastor is to run the organization. He helps the senior pastor keep the staff happy, maintain the church's vision, and sustain its forward momentum.

While serving in that role, my friend attended a conference in Colorado Springs that was geared toward executive pastors. The idea was for guys to meet and compare notes on what was working in their churches and share ideas for improving things.

When my friend arrived, he was aghast at some of the seminars being held. One session promised to show how to increase your church's attendance, raise more money for building projects, and increase giving from your members.

At the time, my friend was in seminary. When he described the session to his professor, the prof was outraged. He blurted, "They might as well call it 'Bodies, Bricks, and Bucks!'"

If this sounds familiar, maybe you've attended similar seminars—*if you're the franchise owner of a Subway or Baskin-Robbins!* How on earth did the principles of business growth find their way into the mission of churches?

The Corporate Model—a "Neutral" System?

You may say, "Hey, it's just a system. It's a way of doing things. Every church has to have that in place."

I agree. But we haven't been very good at examining the negatives of the corporate way. How, exactly, does it affect a church's true mission? For example: Does a "success/growth" model encourage serving each other? Does it encourage reaching out to the community in humility and sacrifice?

The vast portion of energy in a corporate model goes toward operational stuff, such as construction and staff. After all, you have to accommodate your influx of new spiritual consumers. That isn't bad in itself. But have we subtly replaced a transformational and missional focus with physical structures? What happens to the values and virtues of the Sermon on the Mount? Can your church be known as "servant to all" when its drive is to be "bigger and better than before"?

Here is where the conflict becomes real. Christian Schwarz,

of Natural Church Growth Discipleship Resources, writes about where the church takes a left turn. He says the corporate mentality pushes a church's *secondary virtues* ahead of its *primary virtues*:

> My criticism of some sectors of the church growth movement has been that they focus too strongly on secondary issues such as management techniques, marketing methods, analysis of contextual factors, numerical goal setting, etc. Secondary virtues aren't bad things, but they should never be confused with primary virtues such as passionate spirituality, empowering leadership, or loving relationships. Once the primary virtues are highly developed in a given church, we might tackle some of the secondary virtues as well, but they still will be—theologically, spiritually and strategically—of secondary importance.[1]

Maybe today we're getting what we asked for with a success-driven mentality. When the secondary replaces the primary, we pay the price for our choice—literally. And right now, the landscape is littered with heavily-mortgaged churches that have been shuttered by their huge debts.

Yes, we bought it—and now we're paying for it.

So, have we asked God what he thinks about it all? And have we sought him for guidance on how to reverse the trend?

It's time we do.

---

[1] Christian Schwarz, *The 3 Colors of Love: The Art of Giving and Receiving Justice, Truth, and Grace* (St. Charles, IL: ChurchSmart Resources, 2004), 41

One-Minute Reflection:

Do your church's leaders operate in a shroud of secrecy?

Is your church's standard of "success" based more on Scripture or on the world's ideas?

chapter 18

THE "BASTING" PRINCIPLE

CEOs rarely take an issue before the masses for approval. It just isn't efficient. It's much easier to push an agenda dictatorially.

I've seen up close how some church leaders accomplish this kind of push. They use a technique I call "the basting principle." Here's how it works.

Let's say there are questions in the air over the church's direction. Rather than field those questions and face them head on, leaders choose a strategic "distraction."

Now, what is the easiest way to distract a church? Its distinctives! Those things that spark a passionate response among the people. Suddenly, compelling phrases are repeated from the pulpit, like, "We're a church that stands on the Word of God. And we won't waver an inch." Tell me, who wouldn't agree with that?

But watch out! *This is the basting principle at work.* The pastor starts ladling over people's heads certain "juices" that elicit their compliance. These juices distract them from the thorny issues the pastor doesn't want to deal with. And it all plays out very effectively.

How the Basting Principle Works on You

Let's say you're a regular guy, and you're having concerns about your church's direction. Week after week, you hear the same phrase being invoked: "At this church, we stand on God's Word. And we won't waver an inch."

You look around and see everyone basking in the message. It's comforting to know your church is close to God's heart. *That's right, we at First Church of Such-and-Such are held up as the best of the lot. We're a people whose every action is based solidly on the Word of God. Every other church be accursed—we won't fail to uphold God's truth!*

Have you ever seen this happen? People sit in the pews like turkeys in an oven, unaware they're being cooked. Meanwhile, the message they hear is like juice squirted from a turkey baster. The more the pastor squirts on them, the more they love it— because it makes them feel better there in the hot oven.

"Yes, give us more," they say. "This is the truth we want to hear, again and again." They think they're being given what they need. But the whole time, they're being cooked at a hotter temperature!

Ed Galisewski

Squirming in the Pews

Now, back to you in the pew. What about all those questions you wanted to raise about the church's direction? What happens to your concerns in this kind of environment?

As you look around, nobody else seems to share your worries. They're all reveling in the basting juices of "truth" being poured over them.

In the next row, you see a buddy of yours. You talked with him just last week, and he had the same concerns as you. But now he's nodding, "Yes, yes," at the message coming forth. He doesn't look concerned—he looks perfectly content. What happened?

Maybe now you're hesitant to raise those questions you had. If your church is all about standing on God's Word, does that mean you don't stand on the Word? Are you missing the boat? Questions pop into your mind: "Why am I so concerned about things here, when nobody else is? Am I off base?"

Now you're in turmoil. But I tell you, you're not alone. You can bet the same thing is happening in other Christians around you. If you've ever been put in this position, see if your thinking went like this: "If I raise a question, will I be seen as working against God's will? I've seen others ostracized for taking stands like mine. Those people are long gone now. I can't imagine leaving this church. If I don't belong here, where will I go? It's the only place I know that stands on God's Word. I can't give up my purity of belief.

"I guess that settles it. I'll stay where God's Word is supreme. I'll just have to reconcile my questions somehow. I'll trust God to work things out. At least I'm in the one place where I know his Word is being honored."

Unfolding Just as Planned—by the Leaders

Do you get what's happening? I can tell you with authority:

Your leaders are banking on your having those very thoughts. So they keep ladling on another coat of comfort, in the form of a familiar distinctive.

Now you, the questioner, end up basting in the juices being ladled over your head. And the weekly rhetoric keeps coming, to simmer down all your objections. You've successfully placed your turmoil on the backburner. Just as your leaders planned!

And so an important voice is silenced. You only wanted to do right by God's Word. But with enough ladling of self-righteous virtues over your head, your concerns are overridden.

That's the way it works. The basting principle keeps good-hearted Christians from raising deeply felt concerns. They're pressured to abandon them, in order to stay in "God's chosen group."

And God's concerns for that church are overridden as well.

How does this cruel, evil cycle get stopped?

One-Minute Reflection:

> Has there been a time at your church when you felt the congregation was being "basted"?
>
> Have you ever squelched your own deeply felt questions because of a pressure-filled atmosphere?

chapter 19

STANDING ON THE WORD—BUT WHOSE WORD?

I saw the basting principle up close in a church where I was once on staff. Something was rotten, questions had been raised, and staffers and elders were leaving left and right.

A sense of uneasiness had grown to the point that it couldn't be ignored any longer. Soon people were leaving the church—trickling out, one by one, week after week. A fracturing had begun. And the lead pastor knew he had to do something about it.

You would think the pastor might call a "town hall" meeting. The church's leaders could air out all questions and have them addressed. But the very opposite happened. The pulpit was commandeered on Sunday mornings for the purpose of *combating* the questions in the air. There was never an opportunity to have a dialogue about them. Instead, every sermon was used to restate the goals of the church. There was a heavy dose of one repeated phrase: "We stand on the Word of God."

I was actually awestruck at the skill employed to pull this off. Everything coming from the pulpit was meant to "handle" us in the pews. And it did. I don't think I'm overstating this—I think the apostle Paul would agree. *It was pulpit-master genius.* The pastor had "invoked the code." He had stirred up emotions and ladled on the juices. And in doing so, *he had silenced all questions.*

He left people with two horrendous choices: Either leave, and be alienated from your faith family, or stay and shut off the voice inside you in order to embrace the pastor's voice.

A Tactic as Old as the Church Itself

This tactic is not a new one in the history of the church. It was used in the very beginning, by Jewish leaders who castigated Jesus for challenging the status quo. Brennan Manning writes in his touching book *Abba's Child*:

> Pharisees who carried religion like a shield of self-justification and a sword of judgment, installed the cold demands of rule-ridden perfectionism because that approach gave them status and control, while reassuring believers that they were marching in lockstep on the road to salvation. Religion became a tool to intimidate and enslave rather than liberate and empower. The Pharisees stirred up the crowd at Jesus' trial with cries of 'blasphemy,' knowing that would hook the crowd into frenzied calls for crucifixion.[1]

Even back then, religious leaders knew how to use psychological pressure to baste the faithful in their own beliefs. Like many before and since, they did it to maintain their power base. *And that should never happen in a church.* If a mission is God-centered, why would its leaders fear legitimate questions? What are they afraid of, if not their own sin?

Paul warns us about these kinds of "fear tactics." And he gives us tools to combat them and the corrupting evil behind it all. He writes, "Those false teachers are so eager to win your

---
1 Brennan Manning, *Abba's Child* (Colorado Springs, CO: NavPress, 2002), 79.

favor, but their intentions are not good" (Galatians 4:17, NLT).

In his Bible translation *The Message,* Eugene Peterson phrases Paul's words this way:

> Those heretical teachers go to great lengths to flatter you, but their motives are rotten. They want to shut you out of the free world of God's grace so that you will always depend on them for approval and direction, making them feel important.

At the Root of It All

At heart, most control-oriented pastors are the same. They're like "The Fonz," that character played by Henry Winkler in the '70s TV series *Happy Days.* Fonzie could never admit he was wrong. Whenever he saw his error, and he wanted to come clean, he began to stammer: "I was wr-wr-wr-o-o-o-o-...I was wr-wr-wr-o-o-o-o-..." He could never bring himself to spit out the word "wrong"!

I believe the corporate model is partly to blame for this attitude. It has created a breed of pastors who control levers from the top. And that taps into the worldly ambitions of men who've been called to serve.

Really, what harm comes to a pastor if he admits he's wrong? *None.* And what good comes to him? *Everything you can imagine*—grace, release, acceptance, growth in his God-appointed role. Now, what good comes to the congregation in all this? They get a Christlike example—of humility, of servanthood, of what it means to mature in faith. In a word: *Everyone grows in the character of Christ.*

Dishonoring Through False Honoring

We actually dishonor our leaders when we believe they're less fallible than we are. Everything in the Bible screams against it. But that's just our nature—our sin nature. We back down in powerlessness before the very people who *should be serving us.*

Yet, what harm is there if we admit to ourselves, "My spiritual leader is imperfect"? Why do we persist in setting up an "anointed entity" in our lives? What makes us give our allegiance to someone other than God?

Are we too willing to give control of our spiritual lives to some leader? Isn't it wrong to give someone power reserved only for God? If so, what drives us to do it?

One-Minute Reflection:

> Do your church's leaders have a hard time admitting they may be wrong?

> At times, have you handed control of your spiritual life to your pastor, rather than to God?

part six

ACTING ON A SIMPLER FAITH

chapter 20

MAKING LIKE TOTO—PULLING BACK THE CURTAIN

When I served the men's ministry in our church, I was a lay minister by training. But I was an unpaid minister by choice.

There was an advantage for me in not taking payment. It allowed me to speak my mind freely to the powers that be. And I never had to fear losing my source of income.

That freedom isn't enjoyed by staffers in control-oriented churches. This was a sad reality for the executive pastor at the church I mentioned earlier, the one where the pastor silenced all parishioners' questions through his sermons.

Power Loops and Plausibilities

This executive pastor was "in the loop" with the top-dog pastor and his inner circle. So this guy was privy to a lot of decision-making. He thought that having that knowledge protected him. After all, knowledge is leverage.

Wrong. In his case, being privy to knowledge of decisions worked in reverse. It worked to protect the pastor—not him!

This is a common setup in the corporate world. A system of delegation is put into place, where the top dog is "privy" to decision-making but not responsible for knowing what goes on. I know—this sounds like doublespeak. (And it is.) But the aim of the system is to maintain a "plausible deniability" so the leader is protected *at all costs*.

The system looks like it protects others in the loop, too. It can work to make them look innocent when they're not. It allows them to make heavy or cold decisions and come out smelling like a rose.

But in the long run, there's no real protection for these underlings. They're always vulnerable to having blame laid at their feet. (Just ask Chuck Colson, the "fall guy" for former President Nixon.) Because when push comes to shove, the top dog is the only one who's guaranteed protection—*at all costs*.

"Do Not Contact"—Three Words That Cause Me to See Red

Back to my executive pastor friend. "Sensitive" information got leaked from the leaders' inner circle. Their convenient scapegoat? The executive pastor. He was fired—and staffers were told he was *not to be contacted* for any reason.

Now, to me, the "do not contact" mode is never helpful. It's the worst scenario you can have. First, you're never able to get to the bottom of what really happened—and that means no healing can take place. People are just left dangling—hurt, resentful, and powerless to do anything about it.

The executive pastor who was fired wasn't innocent by any stretch. But he was my friend. And no way was I going to let the whole thing get swept under the rug—which was the leaders' plan.

The best scenario, of course, was for both parties to come together. But that wasn't going to happen. So I took the bull by the horns. I called up several church leaders, including elders and staff members. I persuaded them to call the ousted executive pastor, to see how he was doing—*and to ask questions about what the hell happened.*

(I'm such a pain in the butt in these situations. I never take "no" for an answer.)

This group of leaders—I'll call them "the investigative team"—rang up the executive pastor. And they got an earful. He filled them in on some important facts missing from the "official version" of his firing.

As I said, my friend wasn't innocent. He had overstepped the bounds of Christ-centered leadership. But during those calls from the investigative team, he owned up to his part of the mess. And he wanted them to know he hadn't acted alone.

A Nickname I Never Wanted

You can imagine how steamed the investigative team was when they heard all this. They came back to the church's inner circle demanding an explanation. Of course, none was forthcoming. The response from leadership wasn't just, "No thanks." The team was told, literally, "It is finished." (Spooky reference, huh?)

The team tried vainly to bring the truth to light. They pleaded for transparency to the congregation—but to no avail. In the end, some just couldn't accept what had gone on—so they left the church. For a few, this meant leaving their church-related jobs. Others who took part in the investigation were "asked" by the inner circle to leave.

When all the dust cleared, something important got revealed. It was something that happens in a lot of churches and ministries: *One man had come to possess too much power.* Power that had never been earned—power he never had the right to possess.

In short, the curtain was pulled back to reveal a lot of lever-pulling. Leaders had created a convincing act to maintain the illusion that everything was okay. It was all just to maintain control.

Sadly, I was given a nickname out of that experience. The staff started calling me "Toto." I was the one who had pulled back the curtain. Believe me, I hadn't wanted to do that. I was mad there was ever a curtain to be drawn back in the first place.

And that's my point here. *There should never be a curtain in a church setting.* Back rooms are for shady corporations to do their dirty dealings—not churches.

Courageous Efforts Versus Comfort

So, what happened to Jesus' message of leaders-as-servants in all this? It was never a part of the conversation. Plenty of "honor your pastor" verses were trotted out, but Christ's thunderous words against abusive religious leaders were never invoked.

In the end, there weren't enough people with the courage to question one man's abuse of power. An honorable group of people had tried. They had been guided by their sense of integrity. But it hadn't worked.

That wasn't what bothered me most, though. It was that so many Christians didn't want to deal with the drape being pulled back. *They wanted to keep things the way they were, because of the comfort it provided.*

There are always courageous souls who try to confront in a godly way. But all too often, there's a barrier blocking their efforts: the congregation itself. We'll look at that next.

One-Minute Reflection:

> How have "dissenters" at your church been treated?

> Have you ever been involved in a church conflict that called you to have courage over comfort?

chapter 21

WE'RE OFF TO SEE THE WIZARD!

Power plays like the one in our church aren't that rare. Why?

Human nature. Mix that with a corporate model and one man's ambition, and you've got a toxic brew.

Let's talk about the human nature part of this equation. Over time in this kind of church, people come to believe the pastor has "wizard-like" qualities. They look to him to provide all direction and guidance. No one admits it, but everybody's default thinking is, "The wizard will know what to do. He'll have the answer for us."

That was the trump card in our situation. The people were too comfortable having a wizard. They were shown the problems at the top, but they didn't want to upset the status quo. They wanted their wizard in place, more than they wanted to solve a problem that grieved God.

It was disheartening. But what amazed me most was that people actually *liked the system*.

A Surprising Source of Lethargy: Us!
A wizard provides comfort. That's one reason a congregation will give him power.

Another reason is the value we evangelicals place on evangelism. Who's the one person thought to be most adept at leading people to Christ? It's almost always the pastor.

A lot of Christians shudder at the thought of witnessing to their "nonbelieving" friends. They'd prefer to bring them to church. They want their friends to hear the gospel preached from an authority: the guy in the pulpit. For that reason alone, the pastor is seen as indispensible.

Scripture says otherwise. God's Word tells us that all believers are part of a holy priesthood—and that means everybody. Too often in evangelical culture, we stop owning our responsibility for living *and sharing* the gospel message.

No believer is a more important voice of God than any other. But in certain churches and groups, the man in the pulpit is looked to as the "sole soul converter."

The Drive to Follow a Cause
Another reason Christians give such power to pastors is they naturally have a desire to follow a cause. And by the very nature of his job, a pastor embodies "the Supreme cause" full-time.

We all want to be part of something larger than ourselves—especially the greatest Cause. But too often, we go overboard by giving all power and decision-making to leaders who take that power and abuse it. Rather than face the hard work of discerning God's agenda together as a church, we act more like lemmings. Instead of *doing* what's right, we prefer to have our leader *tell us what's right*. He ends up deciding the cause—not us as a body.

We long to be basted with our own distinctives: "Yes, another ladle of truth over my head, please!" But that's not going to cut it—for any of us.

I found out firsthand how easy it is to succumb to the "wizard mentality." And it gave me the shock of my life.

One-Minute Reflection:

Do you rely on your pastor's sermons to present the gospel message to your friends?

Does your congregation rely solely on your pastor to discern God's agenda for your church?

chapter 22

RESISTING THE "MESSIAH COMPLEX"

I was asked to lunch by a guy who'd been attending the men's ministry. He was struggling to break a habit of viewing pornography online. As he laid out his problem, he said, "This stuff is so addictive. It's really hard to break." Then he looked at me and said, "But I know you can't relate to this."

"Really?" I asked. "Why don't you think I can relate?"

"Well, you're a pastor," he said. "I know you guys don't have the same type of weaknesses we other guys have. Or the same kind of desires."

I almost fell out of my chair. I not only had the same desires—*I had the same weaknesses!* Yet this guy thought I was above that type of struggle.

That's what threw me most—that anyone would think leaders are beyond lust. Yet, the truth is, *a lot of* Christians hold to this idea.

Clinging to Fallacies About Our Pastors

You may ask, "How could any responsible leader let that kind of fallacy continue?"

I found out how. As the guy continued, he addressed me as "Pastor Ed."

Pastor Ed. The title itself suggests a capable minister. One who can help a struggling man deal with his deep issues. I had to admit, it felt good to be seen that way.

Of course, the reality was, I *wasn't* a pastor. I was just a volunteer lay leader. Or, really, just a guy trying to give other guys a place to be real about struggles and not feel guilty about it.

Yet, in that moment, I saw a temptation for all ministry leaders. It's something that's in front of them constantly. The temptation is: *What a rush! To be seen as able to help—because I've conquered common struggles!*

It was a lie—and I resisted it. In fact, I made a point to tell the guy very specifically about my own struggles. It was this conversation, in fact, that compelled the open confession I gave a few months later at the men's retreat.

Sitting at the table that day, I determined: "I'll be damned if this fallacy continues. I won't let this man—or any man in our church—hold that kind of a lofty view of a Christian leader. *Ever again.*"

From that day forward, I decided, every time I held a microphone in front of a group of men, my message would be this: "You are not alone in your struggles."

"The Messiah Complex"—and Our Part in It

During that lunch meeting, I came face to face with what must be the biggest façade in all of religion. It's the idea that, besides Jesus, there could exist on earth a human being who hasn't struggled with sin.

God forbid! The very thought is heresy.

As I sat across from this guy, I decided to let our exchange be transformational. It was a lesson "in the moment" for that man struggling with sin. But it was just as much a lesson for me. It was something I would carry with me as long as I was engaged in men's lives.

I had seen up close how a "messiah complex" develops. It happens as a two-way street, with both parties contributing. This guy wanted to believe I was above lusting. Maybe he wished that because he wished it for himself—"If he can do it, I can do it." But it was a fallacy.

Tragically, it's a fallacy supported by "group think." We want to believe our leader is above it all. And, together, our group-think supports it. But this particular group-think causes a problem that I think grieves God. *It makes every guy struggling with sin think he's the only one!*

The malady of group-think has plagued the church for centuries. Thankfully, a great philosopher from the Christian ranks helped expose it all—and point us forward.

One-Minute Reflection:

How may group-think in your church support fallacies?

How does it affect you to hear the words, "You are not alone in your struggles?"

chapter 23

AN "AUDIENCE OF ONE"

We're not the first generation of believers to succumb to group-think.

Søren Kierkegaard, the nineteenth-century Danish philosopher, wrote powerfully on the subject. He saw the church's tendency toward group-think as being rooted in man's fallenness.

Kierkegaard said that whenever group-think was practiced, it gave rise to a type of "mob rule." Yes, even inside the church! It allowed groups of Christians to turn against others without feeling any personal responsibility.

What was needed, Kierkegaard said, was to be an individual, not just to acquiese to a group mentality. Vardy summarizes his view this way:

> A person today may be brought up in a Christian culture or may hear the Christian message, but this in itself will not be enough to engender faith. Faith is something that must be accepted or rejected individually. . . . A person cannot live out a subjective relationship merely by being

part of a crowd or a group; each person has to live the relationship as an individual.[1]

This wisdom is so needed today. Why? The "audience of One," as Os Guiness says, calls me to deeper reflection before the Creator.[2] And that, in turn, will lead me to gutsy action—to be willing to expose every divergence from the simplicity of the gospel. Only as I have this one-to-One connection with God can I be involved in community in healthy ways. It encourages me to get involved with others without transferring my allegiance from the Lord to them.

A Word of Reassurance to Pastors

I've been talking a lot in these few chapters about church problems. I need to pause here to offer a word of reassurance to pastors.

I'm on your side. I really am. I'm all about ministry—and have been since day one. I know many of you clergy reading this might feel beat up by all the accusations I'm making. I truly believe the majority of you are doing "good church." But the reality is that if we're not broken and humble and calling on the Holy Spirit to lead us, too often we can go down the path of "bad church." One of the main concepts of this book is to let your congregation keep you accountable. Be humble enough to invite the oversight and scrutiny that can cleanse away any hidden agendas.

Now . . . can we do a little reasoning together? You want to lead a people "who stand on the Word of God." First of all, let me ask you: Are you tempted to think of yourself as "above the fray" when it comes to human weakness? Or maybe you're tempted to cover up your weaknesses?

---

[1] Peter Vardy, *Kierkegaard* (Liguori, MO: Triumph, 1997), 20.
[2] Os Guinness, *The Call: Finding and Fulfilling the Central Purpose of Your Life* (Nashville, TN: Word Publishing, 1998), 73.

Second, are you tempted to see people in your church as troublemakers when they raise honest concerns?

You've read about all the problems that can happen with this sort of mind-set. And you've been given fair warning here—from history, from the Bible, from others' experiences. You yourself have probably seen a trail of decimated souls along "Messiah Complex" Boulevard.

So, what do you make of what you've read so far? And what does it stir in you?

A Word of Reassurance to Parishioners

Now I have a word to offer congregations. I want you to be very clear in your mind on the following:

There is nothing wrong with standing on God's Word to tell leaders that their decisions should be on the table for scrutiny.

There is nothing anti-God about telling a leadership team they need to listen to the congregation about issues the people want addressed.

There is nothing wrong with asking leaders to evaluate whether your church is too dependent on one person. That's a problem that always compromises the health of a group.

I've been around church long enough to learn this: Differing opinions and constructive dialogue lead to the greatest moments in our Christian walk. When we wrestle with issues and don't hold our views so rigidly, we have our biggest breakthroughs for God's glory.

It's not about being right—it never has been. It's about maturing in Christ. And that takes humility—both from the people and from the pastors. Any mission we undertake must always do one thing. *It has to drive us to the foot of the cross, into a posture of raw need.*

What It Means to *Do* Something

Maybe you're wondering, "Is this guy advocating a Lone Ranger faith in this book?" No way. Am I telling you to go it alone? Absolutely not. Am I condemning all denominations as power-hungry? Absurd. Am I calling for wishy-washy faith that doesn't stand on God's Word? To me, them's fighting words.

So we're settled on that.

Now, then—am I critiquing our present way of doing things? I most certainly am. Am I crying "foul" over practices that Jesus and Paul called rotten? You bet I am. Am I saying that doing nothing changes nothing? If that's what you're hearing from me, then I'm getting through.

Now, what does it mean to actually *do* something?

(Gulp.)

It's a tough question. But it can't be avoided. And we're going to address it—together. We've got some inspiring examples from history to show us the way.

One-Minute Reflection:

What does an "Audience of One" look like in your life?

Have you ever seen a grace-filled breakthrough when two differing parties held constructive dialogue?

part seven

THE CALL FOR A SIMPLER FAITH THROUGH HISTORY

chapter 24

UNITY—A RARE PICTURE IN HISTORY

Imagine you were at the Continental Congress at the birth of the United States. In those first sessions, a handful of representatives wanted to abolish slavery. So the gathering put the issue on the table and discussed it.

From the outset, the dialogue was volatile. Tempers shot so high that eventually the representatives couldn't talk about it anymore. The thought of ending slavery at that time was considered too divisive. The Congress left the issue on the table with no progress made.

A century later, slavery still hadn't been abolished. Not only that, it had flourished beyond anyone's imagining. Entire parts of the country had built their economy around enslaving black men and women. Once again the issue was brought to the center of national discussion—and this time there was no getting around it. Slavery was so enormous now, so completely entrenched in our country, ending it was going to have huge reverberations.

But our governing leaders did decide to abolish it. The result was 620,000 American deaths in the conflict that followed. The U.S. Civil War claimed more lives than all other American wars put together up to Vietnam.

In retrospect, I can't help wondering: How much better would it have been to hash out the issue at the very beginning? So what if it was uncomfortable, unsavory, even painful? What if our forefathers had shown some wisdom and scrapped to find the strength to do the right thing at the beginning? Would their efforts have spared more than a half-million lives a century later?

Rare Calls for Unity

I'm not comparing slavery to religious divisiveness. But, like slavery, ugly denominational rifts have flourished for centuries. And we've done next to nothing to repair those rifts. Instead, we've lived with them as if they're not important. If ever there has been a negative impact on the souls of people—and, in earlier times, on their lives—it has come from this issue. Both the church and the unbelieving world have suffered from our doctrinal divisiveness.

Today, friction between denominations is expected. Meeting at the foot of the cross? Are you kidding? Instead of unifying to support each other's pursuit of God, group after group has splintered off—to the point that we have as many as 1,200 in the US today.

And since we're on the subject of divisiveness: Race is as big a division in the church as any other. We're a century-and-a-half down the road since slavery ended, and half a century since the Civil Rights Act—yet Sunday morning is still "the most segregated hour of the week," as Martin Luther King, Jr. put it.

Nine times out of ten, our splintering hasn't been for righteousness' sake. It has been to accommodate man's differing ideas (and demands) on "the" way to follow God. On rare occasions, someone has taken a righteous stand for the sake of people's souls. But most splintering has come about because leaders locked horns over a doctrinal issue of marginal worth. When they didn't come out of the argument on top, they just walked away. And they started a whole new group fitted to their view of things.

This ugly, pathetic cycle in our history continues to repeat itself. Down through the centuries, few voices have rallied to preserve unity in the body. How many biographies have you read where a Christian leader took a stand by saying, "All this division is unhealthy. It runs counter to the cause of God. It moves us farther away from Christ's desire for us. It's time for us to repent and act according to his will. That means coming together in unity and love. I'm issuing a call to set aside our differences, so we can glorify God as one."

Not a very popular rallying cry, is it? After all, it doesn't name a convenient enemy. And it doesn't baste us in the juices of superiority over other groups.

Rare Acts of Unity

Since the beginning, division has never been part of God's plan for his church. His desire all along has been for a people to unite in his name, and together to promote his purposes on the earth.

The book of Acts is a vibrant case in point, where all the believers in Jerusalem came together for the common good: "They devoted themselves to the apostles' teaching and to the fellowship, to the breaking of bread and to prayer. Everyone was filled with awe, and many wonders and miraculous signs were done by the apostles. All the believers were together and had everything in common" (Acts 2:42-44).

As the church spread throughout that region of the world, conflicts certainly arose. But the apostle Paul dealt head-on with every divisive issue of his time. Again and again, Paul preached charity, forgiveness, and generosity in his letters to the churches he founded.

Paul always refocused the issue on Christ—on the cross, on common faith, on loving each other sacrificially. He specifically called for the body to align under the Head—Christ himself. Paul didn't beat around the bush on this topic. He meant business, speaking boldly with authority. Even when Paul himself was a source of disunity—parting ways with Barnabas over his nephew John Mark—Paul eventually sought reconciliation.

More Convenient to Divide Than Reconcile

It's amazing how many issues there are to potentially divide us—and that *have* divided us over the centuries. Rituals of baptism, speaking in tongues, abstaining from meat, pacifism, the role of icons. As we deal with matters like these, we continue splintering off into multitudes of sects. Why?

It's been convenient. Yet with every split, the gospel becomes more and more obscured. Our sacrificial acts in God's name become less and less effective. Meanwhile, the world sits back and shakes its head in disgust.

For the sake of the gospel, we have to look at these continuing divisions with greater concern. We need a sense of urgency to correct all the fracturing. Otherwise, the road we're on will splinter into more directions with each succeeding generation.

Rare Critiques Regarding Unity

As people of various Trinitarian faiths, we agree on the essentials. It's our marginal differences that build barriers between us.

Think about it. It's not the Creator-Savior-Guide aspect that causes us to disrespect each other. It's not the Trinity that comes between us, negating all possible fellowship and partnership for the gospel's sake. It's almost always points of lesser doctrine that divide us.

We'll only begin to approach Christ's desire for us as we set those differences aside. And that will happen only as we unite in our common belief in and passion for our Creator-Savior-Guide. That's when we'll start to experience true fellowship in love. We'll become a picture of unity. And our impact on the world will be worthy of what our God deserves.

Our Track Record on Unifying
So, how good are we at unifying across denominational lines? Can't think of any good examples? Neither can I.

I can think of some questionable ones, though. Whenever I've seen different denominations trying to join efforts, it hasn't been for the sake of unity in Christ. The goal isn't fellowship, worship, or sacrificial service. Instead, it's usually for some cultural or political aim—in other words, something secular.

Once the issue passes, the various groups go their separate ways, returning to their distinctives. And guess what? They recharge their old hostilities against each other. In short: *It was all for nothing,* if measured by biblical standards. None of the groups came together *for the sake of being together in Christ's name and love*—as he prayed for. Our efforts rarely end in dissolving denominational barriers.

Rare Change
I'll say it again: I'm not proposing some new way to do church. I don't even have a new way—and if I did, I wouldn't trust it. Besides, trying another "way" would only add to the problems.

My goal here is simple: It's to call all believers to do what we can to put a halt to the denominational divisiveness—and start some healthy dismantling.

As for the insanity behind it all, it's too big a problem. Only God himself can put a stop to that. But we can do something simple. *By becoming simpler, we can become more unified in Christ.*

Our God has blessed us with a common bond in him—a bond he empowers with his Spirit. That bond has the potential for so much good. Yet we interfere with it continually, undermining his purposes for us. Why? How does all the fracturing come about?

Hero worship, pride, and unquestioned authority have undermined religion for two thousand years. And the plague continues. We need to look at how all the manmade stuff came about—how this crap has interfered with God's purposes—and what we can do to purge it.

I have to warn you: You may recognize some of these tendencies in your own church. You may also recognize them in yourself. So it may be pretty uncomfortable.

But don't worry. It's the Holy Spirit's job to shine a spotlight on these things in our lives. His desire is to set us free, without condemnation, to be about his agenda.

Let's journey together now, to see how these pitfalls to unity come about.

One-Minute Reflection:

> When was the last time you heard a respected voice in the Christian community calling for unity among believers?
>
> How might "becoming simpler" work to bring unity in Christ's body?

chapter 25

THE RUNAWAY CONGA LINE

When I was growing up, there was a TV skit my family loved. It got used in so many shows and various settings that I'm sure you've seen it. It's the joke of the *runaway conga line.*

You know how it goes. A large group of people are celebrating at some event—say, a wedding reception. Somebody starts a conga line and everybody joins in, following the person in front of them. It's such fun that soon the bride and groom and all their family and friends are involved.

The shimmying line grows so long that soon it starts to circle around on itself. As the people dance away, they begin to wonder where the front of the line is. Everybody loses track of both the beginning and the end—and they start to wonder where they're headed. As they look around, they don't recognize anybody in the next line over. They're not even sure it's the same conga line as theirs!

Now they start wondering, "What happened to that small, fun line with the bride and groom?" But nobody gets out of line—they just keep cha-cha-ing away. The idea is that if one person breaks the chain, the whole thing will fall apart. And nobody wants that blame.

Just ahead, the line starts heading out the door of the reception hall and into the street. Now everybody's wondering, "Where on earth is this taking me? And how much longer should I hold onto the person in front of me?" Still, nobody steps out of line.

People start worrying. One guy shouts to another, "Hey, let's get out of this." But his buddy, with a crazed look in his eye, says, "No, no, don't break the line. Whatever you do, keep going!"

Of course, in the skit this lends itself to all sorts of absurd situations. People conga across heavy traffic, through restaurants, into club meetings, even funeral homes—all sorts of inappropriate settings for a goofy conga line to be shimmying along.

It ends with everybody dancing through a seedy part of town, surrounded by all sorts of shady dealings. Yet, despite the situation, everybody congas on. Eventually somebody shouts, "Hey, shouldn't we stop and get back to the wedding?" But everybody still has that frenzied look. "No, no. Whatever you do, don't step out of line!"

Revealing a Universal Truth
So many situations in life are like this conga line. And the one unchanging rule is, "Don't break the line, no matter where it takes you!"

The skit is so funny because it reveals a universal truth about human beings. Deep down, we each tend to think things will go better for us if we stay in line. If we just focus on the person in front of us and don't look at our surroundings, we'll get where we need to go just fine.

But there's also a more disturbing truth at work in the conga line. That is, *people won't stop even when they know they should*. They know that what they're involved in is leading somewhere wrong—but they're too scared to let go.

Of course, all these little truths translate easily into our religious traditions. If we always stay in line and don't look around, we may *think* we're safe. But we can end up in situations that are laughably absurd—as well as heartbreakingly tragic.

How does this happen? It's when we fail to continually evaluate *the things we hold sacred and important from generation to generation*. All religious groups have established certain practices and rituals. And nobody wants to be the first to break those traditions. If they do, there's almost always a price to pay—and the price is always high.

Traditional Practices—Started by Man
Within every denomination, the traditions in place were started by men. Somebody decided a certain practice was important to do, so that practice got put into place.

Those leaders certainly thought they were following God's Word, in order to do his will. But today, when a group's leaders are pressed to find the age-old practice in Scripture, they can't. So, why continue it?

"We've always done it that way," is usually the answer. "It's part of our identity. It's been built into us over hundreds of years. Who are we to question what our ancestors did? They sacrificed so much to live by this doctrine. We can't treat their sacrifice lightly."

That's one way traditional practices get blindly accepted. And it's a perfect example of *the conga line.*

Our Tendency to Exalt the Wizard

Another way these practices continue is *we exalt our leaders rather than respect them.* From the beginning of time, we've wanted to lift our leaders above infallibility. The trouble is, *it doesn't work in the universe God created!* And it doesn't reflect God's original purpose in giving us leaders.

The best biblical example of this is when Israel wanted a king to rule over them. They wanted to be like the other nations, which had kings. But this grieved God to no end. His being Sovereign over Israel wasn't sufficient for them. His faithfulness to his people just didn't scratch the itch they had.

Tell me, does this sound familiar? Didn't Israel want a "wizard"? Having one would make things a lot easier. A king would make all their decisions for them. That way they wouldn't have to follow God's voice on their own.

In the end, God gave Israel what they wanted—in Saul. We all know how that went.

Israel was used to having God lead them whenever they went to war. God himself gave them all their directions for battle, by speaking through the prophets. But now Israel had Saul as its leader. And Saul's first act as commander in chief was to disobey the directions God had given to the prophet Samuel. It ended in disaster.

God's Word couldn't be clearer about the danger of wanting a "wizard" to lead us. Still, we clamor for one in every generation. It's a temptation that will never go away. This means every generation will have to fight hard against it.

Early Signs of the "Wizard Mentality"

Gregory of Nyssa (AD 330–395) was a great writer in the early church. I thank God for his role in shaping the faith as we know it. But Gregory was also immersed in the "wizard" mentality. This attitude gave rise to a flawed system that persisted for centuries.

Gregory wrote something that reveals the roots of this attitude in the early church. As he describes the ordination of priests, check out how these words can contribute to the "wizard" mentality:

> The same power of the word makes the priest venerable and honorable, separated. . . . While but yesterday he was one of the masses, one of the people, he is suddenly rendered a guide, a president, a teacher of righteousness, an instructor in hidden mysteries.[1]

You can see how the system was set up to fail from the very beginning.

Don't get me wrong here. I have a lot of respect for those who serve in ministry. It's a life choice. You spend your years serving others, tending to their hurts and needs. And I'm sensitive and appreciative about the sacrifice that requires. Such people deserve our respect and, yes, our admiration.

Yet two problems come with giving our clergy a kind of blind allegiance. We need to take heed to avoid both problems:

First, we need to be careful not to elevate any human being. *All* have fallen short of the glory of God. This is both theological doctrine and practical fact, proven in every generation.

Second, if the body of Christ were to share in the ministry of caring for others, those who do it full-time would not have to carry so much of the burden. And they wouldn't be so prone to accepting our blind allegiance. Besides, the number of caring

---
1 Gregory of Nyssa, "On the Baptism of Christ: A Sermon for the Day of Lights" (http://www.newadvent.org/fathers/2910.htm, accessed 07/08/2011).

"ministers" would expand vastly, blessing the needy. And we would receive a blessing in return, by acting as God's ministering hands.

The Early Church's Example of Fellowship

The first-century believers approached ministry with these things in mind. There wasn't a cut-and-dried hierarchy as there is today. Instead, the movement was much more communal, meeting in houses and smaller gatherings.

Long before Christ's followers were ever known as Christians, they were called people of "The Way." This is because of *the way they lived and ministered to each other, and to their communities*. These believers developed a powerful reputation for their Christlike love for those around them.

Clearly, the early church had it correct at the outset: They loved the Lord their God with all their heart, soul, mind, and strength—and they loved their neighbors as they loved themselves. As Jesus said, *Here, in one sentence, are all the laws and commandments—all the obligations of the Christian life.*[2]

Of course, at that point in history, the professional model of ministry hadn't yet been born. (We do see some of its beginnings in Paul's writings. He laid out the conditions for becoming a pastor or elder, and he urges everyone to support his pastor financially in his vocation. But that's pretty much it. Beyond that, you'd be hard put to find in Scripture a picture of today's church-as-profession.)

In those first few centuries, the church was simply the body of Christ gathering together wherever they could, without being persecuted. Normal people within these gatherings stepped up into leadership roles based on their gifts, whether it was hospitality or teaching.

So it shouldn't surprise us how Peter summed up the concept

---

2   Matthew 22: 37-40 (my paraphrase).

of leadership. He had overseen the church for years when he wrote the following to Christian pastors: "Shepherd the flock according to the will of God, not lording it over those allotted to your charge, but proving to be examples to them" (1 Peter 5:2-3 NLT). Quite a contrast to how we view our pastors' roles today!

The Advent of a "National" Church

Peter's view of leadership—where the pastor is a servant-example—eventually went by the wayside. It happened when the great conqueror Constantine was converted. As a government and military leader, Constantine sought to honor God as he knew how. To him, it meant making Christianity the official religion of his empire.

But when Constantine did this, he allowed his own ambition to seep into the church. Suddenly, bishops were no longer just religious figures. They were political and governmental authorities.

The ripples from Constantine's decision are still being felt today, in ways too far-reaching to describe here. But authors George Barna and Frank Viola have written a great book on the subject called *Pagan Christianity?* They track how a lot of the church's development wasn't always grounded in Scripture. It got corrupted along the way by moves like Constantine's.

For Christians living in Constantine's day, this national Church was the only option around. So, every doctrine that came out of it was a matter of, "My way or the highway." If you challenged a doctrine of the church, you were branded a heretic. In short, you became an enemy of both the church and the state. And nobody wanted to face the consequences of that kind of branding.

Seeking Reform on a Large Scale

As the centuries passed, more and more manmade things crept

in. It's easy to see how that would happen, with bishops being influenced by political and nationalistic needs. The guys who didn't run wild with power still faced a lot of pressures from the government.

Finally, in the sixteenth century, Martin Luther came on the scene. Here was a man who sought to undo some of the corrupt things the Roman Catholic Church had allowed.

Luther had a great passion for God. As a priest in charge of people's spiritual lives, he saw how some church rituals actually led people *away* from their Creator-Savior-Guide. The practices also ran counter to what he saw in Scripture. The sale of "indulgences," for example—a way for people to be granted forgiveness for their sins—was contrary to the free grace of God. Then there was the hierarchy of priests, cardinals, and popes. It all cut across the grain of the early church's community-oriented example.

So Luther famously nailed his 95 theses to the door of the cathedral in Wittenberg, Germany. It was a call to dialogue about these issues. But, of course, there was no dialogue. This unknown priest was going up against the most powerful organization the world had ever known. Yet what Luther said caught people's imaginations. And it caused a full-scale revolution. Instead of dialogue, a literal war broke out.

In spite of the warfare, we can be glad Luther went forward with his challenge. It changed the way faith was lived out, both communally and individually. And it revealed two things that go hand in hand: (1) how off-base man can become over time without examining and rectifying his religious practices. And (2) how difficult and costly it is to face down existing power structures!

In a sense, we still face barriers like Luther's. There's a twofold task in front of us: (1) We have to convince our brothers and sisters how off-base we've all become in some practices, and (2) we have to face down the existing power structures in the church.

So, how do we do this?

The first thing we have to do is tackle the "sandbox mentality."

One-Minute Reflection:

> Where do you see a "conga line" among Christians you know?
>
> Where do you see a true Martin Luther at work today, doing battle against bad spiritual practices that harm people?

chapter 26

LANDING IN THE SANDBOX

When our kids were very young, Lynette and I read a book to them every night called *Brown Bear, Brown Bear*. The book is so repetitious it drove us to insane laughter. But every night our kids demanded to hear it. Page after page, the book poses one question and a changing answer:

> *Brown bear, brown bear, what do you see?*
> *I see a _____ looking at me.*

On every page, the blank lists a different thing. Each thing names something else looking back at them. And it goes on and on and on.

I often think of that book when I consider how the nonbelieving world looks at God's church. In this version of the book, the blanks would be filled with thousands of wildly different groups claiming to present the right picture of Christ. It would just go on and on with things like:

World, world, what do you see?

I see 1,200 groups fighting each other and evangelizing me.

I see groups that dismiss each other and point out the others' errors, evangelizing me.

I see no harmony among Trinitarian faiths, evangelizing me.

I see man in control of each group, evangelizing me.

I see massive amounts of energy spent keeping groups apart, evangelizing me.

I see thousands of groups offering a witness to the world but ignoring others as partners, evangelizing me.

It's an absurd picture, of course—especially to the world, who's on the receiving end. But I think this book should be read by every Christian. And it ought to end with a prescribed prayer:

Lord, I need to see something that resembles your original intention for your followers here on earth. I need to picture a place that helps all believers focus on you—our Creator, our Savior, our Guide. Help us figure this out, Lord, so that all our attention and energy can go toward your business and not ours.

The Sandbox Mentality

The book I imagine is the result of something I call "the sandbox mentality."

You know what happens when one kid doesn't like another kid's rules for play. The first kid declares, "If you won't play my way, I'll go play somewhere else." Then he gathers up his toys and leaves. And he takes his friends with him.

I find the sandbox to be a pretty good metaphor for *the curse of denominationalism*. To me, this curse, more than anything else, erects walls that keep us alienated from each other. And it excuses Christians from not taking seriously Jesus' prayer for a united church.

We know that most denominations were created from man-made doctrines, not from core issues of faith. Some began by emphasizing one nonessential over another. Some came about because of personality conflicts or power struggles. Yet, no matter what their origin, the splintering of the church was never God's original plan for us.

From Conga Line to Freedom to Sandboxes

I would be remiss if I didn't say denominations *have* played a positive role in church history. I thank God someone like Martin Luther was willing to break the conga line when people were heading in a destructive direction.

Plus, church leaders didn't used to "agree to disagree." Instead, they took it out on each other pretty harshly. In certain cases, this was actually deadly. If you disagreed with the official doctrine, it could cost you your life. After all, there weren't a lot of denominations to choose from then.

Things started to improve a bit after the Reformation. But first, there was the bloody Thirty Years War (1618–1648), which was fueled by religious disagreements. Thankfully, a godly man named Meldenius stepped forward with some wise words for disagreeing believers. His compassionate wisdom is still quoted four centuries later: "In essentials unity, in non-essentials liberty, in all things charity."[1]

Church leaders saw the need to adopt this saying. And slowly they began to "agree to disagree" on doctrinal matters, without bringing violence on each other. So the idea of differing denominations was, in a way, a source of mercy. Denominations provided refuge especially for questioners and the disenfranchised. As long as you could agree on the core issues—the Father, Son, and Holy Spirit—it became less important how you practiced baptism, offered communion, or observed worship.

Today, we no longer burn each other at the stake or have the power to excommunicate each other. But how we treat each other *in our hearts* can be just as deadly, in terms of relationships. If we're going to apply what Christ said about the mark of a true Christian—having "love for one another, as he has loved us" (see John 13:34)—then we have to conclude that not many are true followers of Christ.

So in history, breaking from the conga line brought precious freedom. And that freedom brought theological diversity. But our old nature eventually crept back in—and we've misused our freedom to selfishly splinter off. Our arrogant splintering continues to this day.

How Did We Come to This?

Something happens to us in our early years that fuels this

[1] http://www9.georgetown.edu/faculty/jod/augustine/quote.html, accessed 07/25/2011.

arrogance. It begins with our own denominational upbringing.

Think about it. As a child, you were exposed to your denomination alone and the practices surrounding it. It never crossed your mind to try another expression of faith. And nobody from your denomination ever suggested you try something else—it was pretty much unheard of (unless they were trying to get rid of you!).

I know that, as a young Catholic, I would have let my family down if I'd tried another branch of Christianity. Opting out just wasn't part of the picture. So, in a real way, we're all indoctrinated early on by our family's denominational mind-set (even if they don't know they have one).

Things start to shift a little in our teenage years. We naturally start to question everything, because we're beginning to form our adult identity. Part of the maturing process is to pull away from our families to find out who we are as individuals.

For any teenager, questioning your faith is a part of this process. But if you question your faith too much, you get "the stare." I'm talking about the pressure from adults not to raise too many questions—or else. In some cases, this isn't just parental pressure—it's "spiritual" pressure, too, put on us by our faith group. Suddenly, questioning things isn't just a matter of disappointing your family. It's about risking eternal damnation.

But here's the thing about questioning. For teenagers, it's not just natural—*it's essential*. At some point, the faith we inherit from our family has to become our own. And that only comes when you discover and establish your own relationship with God.

Unfortunately, a lot of questioning teenagers experience more than their share of "the stare." And that's enough to make any normal kid want to make a run for it. Or, maybe their personality is on the meek side. In that case, they may question things internally—but outwardly they go along with things just to survive, until they can move out of the house and strike out on their own.

It's during this crucial time—the teenage years and the period just afterward—that most young people make decisions that hold for a long time—sometimes a lifetime. Most either explore other options for faith or reject religion altogether. Of those who walk away, many stay away. But a lot of others never lose their deep yearning to reconnect with God.

Insights from Research

LifeWay Research gives some helpful insights into this pattern. Their study shows that seven out of ten young adults ages 18-22 stopped going to church for at least a year.[2] Evidently, the church they've known isn't enticing enough to keep them engaged.

This is also where many disconnected adults get stuck. If they want to reconnect with their faith, they may try a different denomination from the one they grew up in. But soon they see that the new group they've joined has its own set of rules. To these seekers, it confirms what they've suspected all along: Church isn't really about knowing, loving, or serving God—it's about manmade add-ons. So they give up on church altogether.

But what about those disconnected adults who stick it out? Those who are so determined to reconnect they don't quit, even when they run into manmade barriers?

Rodney Stark's book *What Americans Really Believe* tracks these believers' patterns. His research shows that 44 percent of American Christians have changed denominations. And many do it more than once.[3]

The upshot? We've become a nation of church-hoppers. That's how we deal with dissatisfaction over denominations.

---

[2] "LifeWay Research finds reasons 18- to 22-year-olds drop out of church" (http://www.lifeway.com/ArticleView?storeId=10054&catalogId=10001&langId=-1&article=LifeWay-Research-finds-reasons-18-to-22-year-olds-drop-out-of-church, accessed 07/28/2011).

[3] Rodney Stark, *What Americans Really Believe:New Findings from the Baylor Survey of Religion* (Waco, TX: Baylor University Press, 2008), 21.

If we can't reconcile things, we just keep moving—and moving and moving and moving.

How Family Becomes Adversaries

All this church-hopping creates a competition between denominations. But the competition isn't for converts—it's for the allegiance of believers. Instead of becoming more Christlike as a body—serving the community and each other—denominations get sidetracked creating strategies to "increase membership."

What's the easiest way to gain more members? It's to bring in Christians by advertising the "right set of beliefs." Nobody writes better—or funnier—on this subject than C. S. Lewis, the great Christian writer of the last century. In his book *The Screwtape Letters,* a demon offers advice to his nephew on how to trip up the Christians assigned to him. The best way, says the uncle, is to stir the pot of animosity between denominations. He writes:

> It isn't the doctrines on which we chiefly depend for producing malice. The real fun is working up hatred between those who say "mass" and those who say "holy communion," when neither party could possibly state the difference between, say, Hooker's doctrine and Thomas Aquinas', in any form which would hold water for five minutes.[4]

Lewis hits the nail on the head. Some denominations are dead set on making their differences known so they can appear superior to others. But most of the time, they don't even know what their distinctives are founded on!

That's competition at its crudest. But it's required for any faith group to make their add-ons appealing. Lewis gets to the heart of this absurdity as well. His devil writes:

---

4   C.S. Lewis, *The Screwtape Letters* (New York, NY: Macmillan Publishing Co., 1961), 75.

> What we want, if men become Christians at all, is to keep them in a state of mind I call "Christianity And." You know—Christianity and the Crisis, Christianity and the New Psychology...Christianity and Faith Healing...Christianity and Vegetarianism... If they must be Christians, let them at least be Christians with a difference. Substitute for the faith itself some Fashion with a Christian colouring. Work on their horror of the Same Old Thing.[5]

Denominations think of their add-ons as necessary distinctives. But Lewis exposes that kind of emphasis for what it is: the devil's work!

All the competition between denominations might seem silly to you. But it does do a kind of devilish work. For one thing, it taps into people's weakness for consumerism. More and more big-box churches rely on compelling "worship productions." Some call their worship leaders "production managers," whose job is to "wow" the congregation. These directors orchestrate "quality performances," light shows, and the latest media used at corporate conventions. They would never admit it, but it's strategic sensory manipulation.

Differences Leading to "High Tension"

There's no getting around the absurdity of this competition. But there's another reason groups can't imagine giving up their differences. *It allows them to create their own standards for pleasing God.*

Rodney Stark writes about groups that create a high degree of tension.[6] This is when churches put so much emphasis on keeping rules that it makes them combative with other groups. They see themselves as warriors for God, the sole upholders of true religion. And they tend to dismiss the Old Guard as the

---
5 Lewis, 115-116..
6 Stark, 30.

"frozen chosen." Really, they ought to have a sign out front that reads, "Does Not Play Well with Others." (Sadly, most of these groups would wear the sign with pride.)

"High tension" groups also turn their members on each other. The group's rules become supreme. And that causes people to monitor each other, so they can judge whether the next guy is keeping up to snuff.

But "high tension" groups aren't the only ones who build up walls. Remember the Old Guard I mentioned in the opening chapters? The lazy, complacent, "quiet" believers who need a kick in the pants to be about God's business? They've also done their part to build up walls of separation with other Trinitarian groups.

A Different Form of Tension

One way the Old Guard has done this is through the "historical Jesus" movement. Some church leaders decided to launch a study to find out who the real Jesus was in historical terms. They concluded that the traditional Christ embraced by the church isn't the real one. Instead, the real Jesus was hijacked by fundamentalists for their own purposes.

This creates a different sort of "high degree of tension." On one hand, the zealous groups claim Jesus as exclusively theirs. On the other hand, the Old Guard says their "deemphasized" Jesus—a hazy figure from history—isn't the zealous believers' Jesus at all.

What's the result of these competing views of Jesus? More division. Each group stakes a claim to Christ's identity and his role in the world. Instead, they could be seeking common ground—at, say, the foot of the Cross, where forgiveness is the heart of Christ for every group. But their stubborn emphasis on "the real Jesus" further divides them. Each group would do better just to make their case and let people decide for themselves.

But they insist on throwing rocks at the other guys.

A Time for "Retrospective Responsibility"
The time has come for all believers, of every stripe, to 'fess up on what we've gotten wrong. We need to ask ourselves: Are we truly moving God's agenda forward? Or just a manmade version of it?

We need to take responsibility for the bad that we've enabled to continue in our lifetime. And that means cutting off the curses that have persisted over centuries. We need to start looking past our ideologies and into the faces of real human beings.

One-Minute Reflection:

How did your "denominational upbringing" fuel division with other faith groups?

Where do you see competition between denominations in your own faith community?

chapter 27

FROM TRANSACTIONS TO RELATIONSHIPS

I once attended a seminar called, "How to Share Your Faith Without an Argument." I was drawn by the title. I thought it meant you don't have to cause a fight whenever you bring up religion with people. But it meant something else completely.

The facilitator had put together a sequence of Bible passages that lay out God's plan of salvation. Our task was to guide nonbelievers through this sequence. At each passage, we were supposed to ask them if they believed what we were showing them. The idea was to have them answer "yes" at each point. If they answered "no" at any time, we were to take them through the passage again—convincingly—until they answered "yes."

It was all meant to bring them to one final question: "Will you accept Christ?" If they answered "yes," your job was done. You'd gotten them where they were supposed to go.

Sounded simple enough. But I grew more uncomfortable as the seminar went on. It was all so formulaic, with nothing personal. Basically, it was saying the best way to present the gospel of Jesus Christ was to take a person through steps A-B-C-D—and then close the deal at the end with their final "yes."

By the end of the seminar, alarms were going off inside me. I realized this went against everything I felt, believed, lived, and breathed about faith. All I could think was, "What about spending a month with the person—taking them to lunch, having coffee, inviting them over for dinner? What about asking them, 'How are you doing? How's your spiritual life? What are your thoughts on God?'"

See, I make my living as a salesman. And I know what a *transaction* is. This seminar was nothing more than that—a "close-the-deal" transaction like you'd see on a used-car lot. And you didn't want input from the person you were witnessing to—you didn't want to know them. You were supposed to get through a gospel presentation *without hearing a word from them*—other than the word "yes"!

I couldn't buy it. Probably because I don't do business that way.

But people were buying it. They *wanted* the formulas. After all, knowing a few steps is a lot easier than loving your neighbor sacrificially.

The Amiable Way

When I took this seminar, it was one of the most popular around. People went nuts for it. Yet it might as well have been called "Five Easy Steps to Becoming a Christian Adding Machine: The Coldest, Most Impersonal Approach to Sharing About a Highly Personal God."

The popularity of that seminar reveals something about us. It shows how willing we've been to buy into the corporatization of the church. And I think that's a sad comment on our choices as Christians.

I've been in sales for twenty-four years, and sometimes I am asked by people I work with, "Ed, what are you going to try to accomplish today? How are you going to set up your first sales call?"

For twenty-four years, my answer has been the same: "I dunno. I'm just gonna let it unfold."

It would be dishonest of me to answer any other way—or to try another way. All I know to do is *go visit people I call friends. To love and respect them.* And, while doing that, to promote my products, so they'll keep their door open to me and my company—*because I believe we have something to help them.*

Of course, I have a general sense of direction for any meeting with a client. There's information I want to get across, and I want to know their wants and needs. Our time together should always be well spent.

But my job is NOT to get a doctor to simply say "yes" to my presentation of a medication. It isn't to take him through a series of yes-or-no questions, with every answer being yes, so that I close a sale. Doctors need to come to their own conclusion about what I'm presenting. My job is to give them all the data and outline the features and benefits.

In other words: *It's all about relationship.* People know if what you're bringing to the relationship is real—or if it's only a setup meant to get their buy-in.

"Relationship" in the Corporate World

As you might imagine, the idea of relationship is a major disconnect in corporate America. It's not taught in MBA programs. My approach is quite different from an MBA-like mindset, and this has always served me well in my sales career. My managers just keep telling me, "Keep it up, Ed. Keep doing what you're doing." They realize that relationships are the most important element of sales.

You might think this would be at the forefront of the church's presentation of the gospel. Not so among evangelicals and other "high tension" groups. Most often, their approach is,

"Let me show you where I need to bring you," rather than, "Let me get to know you and love you." It's an impersonal, corporate approach—*because it's all about the transaction.*

Even corporate America recognizes that personalities come into play in the business transaction. Our pharmaceutical company uses the "Insight" model of personalities, to help identify personality styles in us and in our customers. Mostly this is presented as a sales aid, to fine-tune our selling ability. Four types of personalities are identified:

First, there's *the Driver*. This is someone with a personality that's both analytical and dominant. These are the people who tend to run corporate America.

Second, there's *the Expressive*. This person is high energy, like a game-show host. These people do their job by persuasion.

Third, there's *the Analytical*. This person thrives and operates on numbers and spreadsheets.

Fourth, there's *the Amiable*. These are the folks who basically offer care—people such as counselors, therapists, nuns, and priests.

In a corporate scenario, I'll always be an outcast (or, perhaps an "outlier"—a term of recent vintage, basically meaning someone who breaks the mold). Salesmen are usually Expressives. I'm an Amiable. Salesmen also have a little Driver in them. Not me. The only way I can sell pharmaceuticals is with an open ear and with compassion. It's why I enjoy working with my HIV treaters.

How do you get people to "fall into line" in my business? How do you convince them they should jump into a cookie-cutter mentality? You don't. HIV treaters can't tell their patients to jump into an assembly line. These doctors need to offer patients something they know will help them. Otherwise, they won't last very long in the people-caring business. They always do what is best for the patient. Period.

Translating This into Men's Lives

I had to bring this same mentality into my work as a men's minister. Our church's retreats for men showed why. Every time we held a retreat, a certain conversation repeated itself.

The question would come up, "Are you sharing your faith with your coworkers?" The responses we got almost always reflected a by-the-numbers approach. Somebody would say, "Sure, I share my faith. I used the Four Spiritual Laws with this one guy. But he's Catholic, so he wasn't buying it." At that point, he stopped sharing his faith with the other guy—end of story.

In this man's thinking, evangelism was purely an intellectual exercise. So I would ask a follow-up question: "Are you having coffee with the guy? Are you taking him to lunch? Are you helping him with a project on his house?"

"Well, no. I'm just sharing the gospel with him the way it was shared with me."

I can't tell you the number of times this conversation took place. And it typifies our corporate approach to "doing" Christianity.

After a while, I realized there's been a trickle-down effect from generation to generation. I shouldn't generalize too much here, but we baby boomers tend to follow things the way our parents did, unquestioningly. We may be children of the sixties, bucking our parents' cultural norms. But when it comes to faith, we've toed the line more than anybody. How?

The Four Spiritual Laws are a good example. They came about in the middle of the last century. You can't tell me we have to be restricted to the same approach as fifty years ago. Two and three generations have passed, and it's still being used without modification.

I can't help it—to me, sharing the gospel is about being an Amiable. I know there are certain settings for intellectual exchanges, talks that are persuasive and convincing. But is that where most people really live their daily lives—in their heads? Take a look around—most people are struggling to pay their mortgages, to raise their kids, to keep their jobs. They can't afford to live in their heads. Their lives are grounded in everyday realities that require *touch*, not just *words*.

Trying to "close the deal" is a manmade theology. How do I know this? First and foremost, a sales approach has no intention of sharing a burden, of wanting to know what the other person is going through. It may be willing to say, "God knows what you're going through." But it isn't willing to say, "*I* want to know what you're going through. And I want to help you with that burden."

People are hurting. That's something that will never change. Life is basically a struggle. It's why we need grace, strength, and support—and God so desires to give that to hurting people, *through his body, the church.*

For me, the best approach with a hurting person is always this: "Yes, this sucks. It hurts. I have no idea why it's happening. But I want to walk through it with you. We're going to take some time for you to heal through this."

At some point, that person is going to say, "Thank you for loving me." To me, that's the first step for someone to get to know the Source of all love.

The Modern Phenomenon of Being Born Again

When we share the gospel, we use a lot of terms that seem very personal. But sometimes even those personal terms can camouflage a transactional mind-set.

Here's an example. We know Jesus used the words "born again" to describe how a person enters the life of the Spirit. Suddenly, that person is no longer just a citizen of the earth, but also of heaven. Their name is written in eternity. They now see their life as more than a series of daily events—it is a spiritual reality, with eternal value and impact.

It's not uncommon for Christians to ask each other whether they're born again. It can be a useful reference to describe the concept of salvation. But often what we're really asking is, "Are you truly saved?" It's very subtle. But the concept of being "born again" becomes a standard of whether someone is saved at all.

It might surprise you that the term "born again" wasn't commonly used by Christians until a century ago. It was brought into usage during the tent-revival boom, known as the Second Great Awakening. At the time, being "born again" was just one way of committing yourself to God. It wasn't the only way, by any stretch.

Why am I making a big deal out of this? It's because of the way the phrase "born again" has been used by some evangelicals as a measuring stick. Yes, Jesus said, "A man must be born again"—but he was describing a spiritual truth about human transformation. He wasn't establishing a formulaic means of salvation. The early Christians seemed to know this. Otherwise, the church wouldn't have waited eighteen centuries to use the phrase!

Being "born again" has morphed into a kind of litmus test that Newbies use to size up the Old Guard. But it was never intended to have that "edge of judgmentalism." It was really a personal assessment to ask yourself, "Am I accepting the free gift of salvation through Christ's death on the cross?" Even Nicodemus (John 3:1-18) struggled with this born again concept. Jesus had to simplify it for him and tells him it meant, "Anyone who believes in me will have eternal life" (John 3:16). Nicodemus believed Jesus was the Messiah talked about in the Torah, and put his standing within the Jewish community at risk for it, but he still struggled with the reference about being born again.

Many Old Guard also believe that Jesus was the Messiah. Newbies just need to spend some time with them so they have a chance to ask them and find out, not just judge them. No one should assume people aren't "born again" just because they aren't familiar with the nuances of Newbie-speak.

The Cost of Corporatizing

The cost of corporatizing the church is a human one. I don't think we've begun to add up the tally. What I can tell you, from real experience, is how closely the transactional approach has hit home in my own family's life.

A number of years ago, my mother and father began attending the evangelical church that my wife and I had adopted. As I've already mentioned, my parents raised me in the Catholic faith they were brought up in. They had already been through baptism, communion, and confirmation. Yet at one point, my mother told us she wanted to formally ask Christ to be her Savior and Lord. She had never formally done that in her Catholic experience—it just wasn't the way things were done in that tradition.

But now she saw the evangelical emphasis on this—and it had great appeal for her. So we met with a pastor who explained to her in more depth what she was choosing to do. Mom enthusiastically agreed. (My dad took a pass at the time.) For Mom, doing this was her way of expressing her full surrender to God. Yet it didn't dismiss her Catholic experience, which she still cherished.

Several years later, after my father had passed away, Mom was paralyzed by a stroke. We had to find her a facility where she could be tended by full-time health workers. Thankfully, we were able to find a good one. It even had a faith aspect that has made Mom's time there better.

But one day there was a snag. One of the workers at the facility approached my mother to ask about her salvation. Mom explained her Catholic upbringing, and then the commitment to Christ she made later in our evangelical church. She explained that she had also been baptized, but because she had been in a wheelchair she had to be sprinkled instead of "dunked."

The worker's response was that my mother had to be baptized in the manner prescribed by the worker's church—which was dunking. Otherwise, Mom wouldn't be in heaven.

When Mom heard this, she was distraught to no end. I later had a beautiful and intimate conversation with her about it, and I helped reaffirm her commitment to God through Christ.

But how tragic that she had to endure that kind of man-made crap! It showed me just how clinical, driven, and unfeeling believers can be when denominational doctrine trumps love. Think about it: My mother had expressed to that worker the most important words any believer can say to another: "Jesus died on the cross for me. He is my Savior." Yet when it came to the concept of salvation, her words meant nothing in the worker's eyes. Instead, it was reduced to *a baptism ritual!*

Is it any wonder the world looks on aghast? Yet things like this happen so frequently between believers. Should we be surprised that critics of Christianity have risen up in such great numbers, especially in the past decade?

Later, we'll take a hard look at what the Richard Dawkinses and Sam Harrises of the world have concluded about us. And it won't be easy to hear.

But it won't be the last word, for sure.

One-Minute Reflection:

> Do you approach evangelism as if people need to be convinced of something? Or as if they need to hear Good News?
>
> Do you boil down the concept of salvation to a ritual?

part eight

MOVING FORWARD TO A SIMPLER FAITH

chapter 28

LOOKING AROUND THE BANQUET HALL

When you grow up in New Jersey, you spend a lot of time in banquet halls. All the big events of life happen in these places—weddings, baptisms, first communions, and christenings. From day one, they're part of your life.

As you drive along the routes through Jersey's townships and suburbs, you see these halls dotting the landscape. Inside they're one big room, filled with big round tables and a long main table at the front. Sometimes a VFW or Elks hall is used for the same events. But in the end, it's all about what goes on inside. They're not just a part of the visual landscape, but a huge part of the emotional landscape, too.

Maybe that's why I had a dream one night that took place in just such a hall. It was one of those dreams that comes along every once in a while to tell you something important is going on inside you.

I was sitting at one of thirty or forty tables filling the room. Each table represented a denomination. There was a lot of tension in the air. Each group had its own interpretation of Scripture. And they all looked suspiciously and skeptically at the other tables.

The long main table at the front of this hall was God's. Like the head table at any event, it was situated on a riser, so the honored party could see all the tables.

I couldn't see the Lord, but I knew he was at that table. I wondered what he thought as he looked out at all those tables scattered through the hall. Then an awful feeling came over me. All the different interpretations . . . all the tension it created . . . all the alienation that existed. . . . It wasn't just pathetic. It was tragic.

I looked over my shoulder and saw that other tables were being moved into the room. I knew what that meant: more division, more tension, more alienation.

Maybe you're like me. As you imagine this scene, you think of God's sadness at all the dysfunction between our churches and groups, his body of believers. It could be so different.

Tell me—is it really ludicrous to try picturing everybody at one big table? With God at the head position? What would that look like?

People always come with differences—different personalities, different cultural backgrounds, different flavors of all kinds. Variety is not a bad thing. It enriches us in ways we couldn't enjoy if everything were uniform. It's okay to do church in different ways.

But *variety* is something different from *division*. Variety doesn't lead to judgmentalism and alienation. It leads to celebrating richness—which leads to unity.

We've seen how divisiveness happens. It operates in individual mind-sets as well as large groups. It happens in splintering disagreements that multiply over centuries. And it ends up in two guys arguing in a hotel room when they should be praying together.

In the beginning—at the cross—a single table was set for the greatest of celebrations. Instead, dozens of tables sprang up. Each became a battleship launching torpedoes at the adjacent table. Each positioned itself as different from the others, pitching itself as the best there could be, superior to all the rest.

Let's face it, most Trinitarian faiths would never think of warmly embracing another. They would never think of joining with a different kind of congregation to hold a joint worship service. That just isn't the way it goes. Quite frankly, most Trinitarian denominations bad-mouth each other. They steal from one another. They rally their members, to keep them at their table. And they recruit others to sit down as well.

All for what? Our distinctives aren't faith-builders. They don't usually offer real encouragement. Doctrines can provide peace of mind and comfort to the soul (such as assurance of salvation). Some encourage sacrificial service and spreading the good news. But mostly, doctrinal distinctives are used to reinforce a notion of specialness. They reinforce our *rightness*, our distinctness from the rest. And, in some cases, they help build up a leader's empire.

In short, *distinctiveness* mostly translates into *divisiveness*.

> *I looked around at the other tables. At each one I noticed another person like me—someone with a look of sadness, troubledness, discontent. It dawned on me: Here are others who aren't satisfied with the status quo. Others who must be sickened by all the judgmental division!*

Like me, they were all restless. I saw in their faces a desire to get up from their tables and have a look around the room. So I got up, and others did, too. We all headed toward a staircase leading up to a balcony. Everybody sensed it had the best vantage point for surveying the room.

I lined up with the others to ascend the stairs. When we got to the top, we circled the railing and looked down on the scene below. What we saw was a fractured, broken room. At each table was an awful spirit of arrogance. The people seemed smugly satisfied that their agenda was closest to God's. It created a growing distance, instead of a bridge of common belief.

Nobody was looking in the direction of the head table— only at each other.

I can't help wondering what we've done with our common belief—that of Creator, Savior, and Guide. Paul spoke of breaking down the walls of separation (Ephesians 2:11-18). Have we used our common faith to do that? Has our core belief served to unite us with others in love? Or to continue to divide?

Christian A. Schwarz, the author of *The 3 Colors of Love*, writes eloquently of our tendency to build walls. We begin by objectifying others—and end up dehumanizing them.

> The ability to see the world from another person's point of view doesn't come easily to us. We have to practice it. If we don't practice this art, we will soon see the police as "pigs," demonstrators as "stone throwers," socialists as "atheists," Muslims as "fundamentalists," church planters as "sectarians," charismatics as "demonized," non-charismatics as "unspiritual," Protestants as "heretics," Catholics as "the whore of Babylon." Believe me, meeting thousands of Christians every year in all sorts of contexts, I have collected more of these labels than there are countries in the world. The sad thing is that most people don't even realize that these are expressions of highly ideological thinking—right in the middle of the Christian church.
>
> This is how walls between people come into being. They divide every bit as much as the Berlin Wall divided the city. Of course, anyone who builds such walls will spend a great amount of energy justifying their actions. The Department of Propaganda in their own minds works overtime.[1]

I looked at the others circling the balcony. People were shaking their heads in sadness. Occasionally our eyes met, but no one talked. We just gazed at the tense scene below.

---

1 Schwarz, 89.

After a while, we all looked at each other. We realized we had a common bond. Everybody's eyes showed a passion for something more than our own small table. We knew each table had something to offer all the others. Not only that—we knew we all needed one another.

A lot of people today see the church at a monumental stage in history. Things are in flux.

Baby-boomer Christians are dissatisfied with church. Many are going through the motions. The generations behind them, in their thirties and younger, aren't even interested in church. The latest studies show they believe in God—overwhelmingly so—but they claim no religious affiliation whatsoever. They want nothing to do with organized religion as it exists today.

There's a feeling in the air that change is needed. More and more Christians aren't willing to be one hundred percent in step with their faith group. In fact, a majority want to question old traditions. They think it's time to try new methods of gathering together with other believers. But they're afraid to move forward, because they don't know what it should look like.

If you're one of these believers—and I number myself among them—*you're not alone.* It's right to wrestle with any tradition that's merely an add-on to common belief in the Father, Son, and Holy Spirit.

At one point, we all had the same thought. We knew we had a choice to make.

The first option was to walk down that staircase back to our respective tables and take our seats. But if we did this, nothing would change.

Another choice was to go to the head table—to stand before God and present him with a question: "Are you happy

> with the current state of all these groups living in their little silos? If not, how do we go back to our tables and begin the task of pulling them together?"
>
> I didn't think God was satisfied. I didn't think he was pleased with the current state of a church divided. I believed he wanted to change things—to bring a shift to the fracturing trends of two thousand years.

That's when the dream ended. My fellow seekers and I didn't get an answer from God. But I woke up with a burning desire to ask once more:

What if believers could unite under one simple but powerful expression of faith? What if we could put aside our differences for the greater good? Are there enough people dissatisfied with the status quo to fill up a balcony railing? Are there enough to ask God for his help, to seek to honor Christ's call to unity and love?

Beginning the Journey Forward

That dream was where this whole journey started for me. It told me something important.

There's no better way for us to answer our questions than this: *We have to start talking to Christians outside our church or group.*

The current system has sidelined us. We've all been put in positions that convince us we're helpless. Now it's time we get back in the game. Up to this point, we've been compliant. We've abided by restrictions that were laid down and enforced by man. The question for us now is, "Will I act on what God needs from me?"

Much of the "comfort" we've enjoyed has come from what man has said. But we've found out the hard way: It doesn't bring true comfort at all. Instead, we're restless. As we look around at the way things are, we don't have a deep, settled peace.

I'll say it again, in case it hasn't quite registered: *I am convinced in my soul that God's desire is to have all believers kneeling together at the foot of the Cross.* Only when we come together in true worship—in a spirit of genuine unity—will we know what it's like to live out God's desire for us. And we'll enjoy loving fellowship that isn't possible if things stay as they are.

A Sincere Request
I have a request of you: If you're reading this book, it means you've at least had a passing interest in the subject I'm addressing. Please, evaluate where your group stands in this area of uniting or dividing. If you sense you're being led away from other kinds of believers, rather than toward them—if your church's influence is to distrust other Christians—it might be time to address this in your life.

Healthy leaders in your church will only encourage your quest. If they don't have control issues, believe me, they'll welcome a searching, seeking, honest heart like yours. But unhealthy leaders will question you, stigmatize you, or even pick a fight with you. I've already warned what can happen if you raise concerns.

Our rigid control is folly. And it has done enough damage to the fellowship God wants for us. It's caused enough harm to our witness, and to Christ's prayer for a unified body. It's time we faced down every false belief that keeps us from uniting—and move toward each other in a deep desire to please God.

One-Minute Reflection:

Does your church environment lead you toward Christians who are different from you, or away from them?

What's your first thought when you read this sentence: "What if believers could unite under one simple but powerful expression of faith?"

chapter 29

FREE IN CHRIST!—KINDA

Maybe you have kids who play sports. If so, you know how often conflicts with coaches pop up.

Years ago, one of our children was playing for a husband-wife coaching team, a couple who were acquaintances of ours. Our child was having problems with the wife-half of the coaching unit. As I chatted with the husband one day, I brought up the problem our child was having. I asked if he might relay the concerns to his wife, to see if she could help.

He chuckled. "Sure, I'll bring it up, Ed," he said. "Just like you would bring up something like that with *your* wife."

It wasn't a jab. My buddy was just making a joke. He was referring to the age-old truth that husbands are hesitant to bring up certain issues with their wives. But his message was loud and clear: The best way for us to put the whole thing behind us was to ignore it. It would just go away.

I understood exactly what this guy was saying. It's true that most marriage relationships have constraints in them. Those constraints are predicated on boundaries—some healthy, some not.

But like any parent, I wanted to resolve the tension that was created for my child by this guy's wife. I didn't think ignoring it was the best way to go. The guy and I were friendly enough that I felt I could pursue it with him. So that night I called him. I asked again if he would be willing to reach under the table, where the matter was hidden, and set it on top so it could be dealt with.

We talked for quite a while. In the end, I realized that for him, certain personality traits were at issue. And that issue wasn't going to be addressed in his marriage. Ever.

I'm not critiquing this couple's marriage. I'm just telling you Lynette and I can't operate that way. I understand the need for healthy constraints in any relationship, marriage or other. But when important issues are at stake, ignoring them doesn't work in the long run.

I wasn't willing to keep exposing my child to someone else's "no fly zone." Not without addressing it head on.

Churches: Like Marriages

Churches function a lot like marriages. Some issues are always on the table for discussion. Others never are. When this dynamic is at play, you can guess which "spouse" does the backing off. It's usually the rank-and-file parishioner, not the church leader.

All this is confirmed to me by the churchgoing guys I talk to on airplanes. Most tell me they would love to get together with people from other denominations. They've just never done it.

"Why not?" I ask.

They look startled. "Huh," they say, "I guess I never thought about it." After some pondering, they confide, "I guess people at my church would look at me suspiciously if I brought up the idea. The pastor and leaders, especially. So I just dismiss it. It's not a priority for our church."

Not a priority. *The Lord's final prayer, for his people to be as* one—*on the backburner!*

Wouldn't you say there's a constraint at work in that "marriage"? What's the issue underneath the table? What needs to be brought out and placed front and center?

We need to say it: *A lot of pastors are threatened by the idea of freely mixing with other groups.* After all, if it's allowed, what does that say about the church's distinctives? Its theological rightness? Its calling card as the best church around? Certain distinctives might even have to be set aside!

Pastors establish the status quo—and parishioners go along with it. Mostly, they just want to avoid the blowback that's inevitable if you suggest mixing.

Yet there's another reason for keeping the status quo. With all the chaos of life, we want our church to be a place of comfort. And it should be, in significant ways. We should think of our church as our spiritual home—where we're accepted and rooted, settled in with "family."

But being part of a healthy family means being free to raise concerns. If you have to sit in silence over a deep internal struggle, something important is being held under the table.

The Toxic Cost of "Staying in a Bad Church Marriage"

Are you in that kind of "marriage" with your church? Are you forced to conform to the family's dysfunction? Are you told not to raise questions? Is it deadening your soul?

We've come to the stage in this book where I want to make a bold suggestion. Really, it's the centerpiece idea. The suggestion I want to make is a tough one—but helpful. In fact, for some it will be the only hope of ever recovering from a downward spiral of faith. The good news is, I've known many who have benefited from doing this.

I call it *disengaging*.

I'm talking about leaving your faith group. It may be

necessary, if only for a short while. (Yet few people can know that outcome as they enter the decision.) I suggest it for the sake of salvaging your faith—ultimately, for the sake of your group—and for the sake of Christ's desire for his body.

In no way am I asking anyone reading this to rebel or protest against their current church or group. What I'm offering is a possibility. The idea is to *disengage from your group for a while for your own spiritual health*. Sometimes that's what it takes to be able to regain control of your spiritual life—rather than have it dictated to you.

Making a Healthy Decision
Does your current faith home require you to submit to certain practices or rituals? If so, it may be wise to reconsider whether that group is a good choice for the long-term.

I know from experience that disengaging from your faith home is a hard choice to make. But I can also tell you without qualification: *God desires for you to be in* genuine *Christian community*—not community where manmade tenets are the primary rule. The reality may be that you need to be part of a different community from your current one.

Of course, the very idea of disengaging can strike fear in anyone. You may feel it's not in your interest to stay where you are. You may also feel you don't have the strength to face down the fear of leaving.

I want to help you face down every one of those fears. See, I already know about them. And I can tell you on good authority: *God clears a path for all who have a raw hunger for him.*

One-Minute Reflection:

What issues are "under the table" at your church?

What are your fears about disengaging from a dysfunctional church?

chapter 30

FACING DOWN OUR FEARS

Disengaging from church. We all get a scare when we first think about it. Any sincere believer would. The question to consider is, which of our fears are healthy? And which are not?

For some, it's a fear of being labeled too "casual" a believer—somebody with a watered-down faith. They might even be called a heretic.

For others, it's a fear of being left alone in a desert of isolation. Nobody likes the idea of being cast adrift from community because they rocked the boat.

Still others fear that disengaging would mean disobeying God's command to "not forsaking our own assembling together, as is the habit of some" (Hebrews 10:25, nasb). Where else would they fulfill this command, if not in a structured church?

These are all scary prospects. But we're going to look at how to address them.

For others, a big fear is *losing beloved rituals*. They're afraid if they challenge things, they'll be shunned—and they won't ever get to practice their group's rituals again.

If you fall into this last category, I've got good news: *You don't have to give up anything.*

You like to light candles? You want to use holy water or oil for healing? You like to "lay hands" on each other when you pray for them? You want to pray the rosary?

Do any of these things draw you closer to God or strengthen your faith? Then you should do them. Rituals or sacraments can be a precious part of your walk with the Lord. And, believe me, there's a host of believers out there who have disengaged from their group but still practice meaningful rituals.

Holding onto Your "Thin Place"

Celtic Christians used a term to describe the effect of faith rituals: "the thin place." It's a sense that the veil between you and God in the spirit-realm is paper thin, almost nonexistent.

I myself long to have these kinds of times in the Lord's presence. I love it when I can sense his nearness. Of course, my practices may look very different from yours. But the point is, rituals are not add-ons—*unless.* It's only when they *hinder* our connecting with God—when they become *requirements* to reach some "spiritual standard"—that they become add-ons to God's way.

A book I mentioned earlier, *Pagan Christianity?* by George Barna and Frank Viola, provides a great help. The book looks at the origins of denominational rituals and practices and evaluates whether they're scripturally based or manmade add-ons.

These guys aren't on some witch hunt. They're just offering insights to Christians who struggle on either side of the issue of rituals. Both authors make it clear they don't want to create dissent in the church. And let me say the same, too. I want to encourage you that as you examine the role of rituals and practices in your own life and church, proceed very slowly and thoughtfully.

Opening your heart and mind to other denominational believers may mean being flexible about some rituals, at least *temporarily*. That's probably inevitable, if you're planning to mix with other believers. You may have no choice but to set aside some practices that might conflict with others' ideas of worship. It's easier to do when you've taken time to sort out what's an essential and what's a nonessential.

It's also easier when you're with a group of like-minded, supportive brothers and sisters in faith. This kind of group can take shape, for example, as a lunchtime Bible study—say, a half-dozen people from varying faith traditions. That's what I'm doing right now with my guys' group. It's working wonderfully for all of us—minus our rituals! Those of us who want rituals have found outlets to be able to practice them. (More on this later.)

The point for us is to center our faith and community around the concept of Creator-Savior-Guide—the fullness of God in the Trinity. And to do that, we each have to give up something. If we can't let go of our rituals to do that, then we need to reexamine what those rituals mean to us. And we need to find somewhere else to practice them.

Looking for Others Like You

If this is a dilemma for you, let me suggest something. You might benefit from seeking out one other believer who feels as you do. There can be a lot of comfort when you find out you're not alone.

And, believe me, you aren't. There are many, many others who are just as dissatisfied and alienated as you are. And when you find them—when you're in the presence of a devoted believer who questions things as you do—you'll find the Holy Spirit, your Guide, in your midst. You'll be able to encourage each other in ways that promote growth, discovery, and greater connection.

It was scary for Lynette and me when we first stepped out

of the comfort of our faith community. But the sense of peace and freedom we got from that decision outweighed any residual pain. Saying "enough!" to the "man factor" has been rewarding in itself. It's been life-giving to both of us and even to our kids. We've experienced a walk with God free of any allegiances to a person or system. And we've discovered depth and richness in a wide range of faith communities.

We also began to find others like us. It didn't take long to connect with believers who had a hunger for God—and wanted nothing more to do with perpetuating manmade machinery. I've already mentioned that Lynette and I each currently lead a group—one for men, and one for women. And we're seeing great growth in one another's lives. But we've also seen other groups on the landscape that are providing healthy alternatives. For many, a simpler faith is becoming a reality.

A Final Check of Motives

As we were deciding to disengage, Lynette and I constantly had to check our motives. You will, too.

After we left our group, there were times when I desperately wanted to get back at certain people. Consciously or not, they had made me feel "lesser than" as a practicing Christian. And I felt helpless to do anything about it. My desire to retaliate was unhealthy, no two ways about it. And I held onto that attitude for a long time.

I realized I needed to process those feelings and deal with my anger. I ended up spending a lot of time getting counseling from wise and caring believers. I also spent a lot of time in prayer, asking God to help me forgive them.

It took me about three years to come full circle to a point of healing. Finally, I could say, "I don't blame those people anymore. I blame the system that led to this tragic sad situation."

Then I felt another huge burden lift— when I was able to see *the controlling leaders as victims themselves.* I realized they were only living out a tradition that endures to everybody's misfortune. These guys were yoked with a burden from generations past. And they hadn't broken free from that yoke.

Our Ancestors' Desire to Break Free

I'm sure many of our ancestors felt as we do. Surely there were those who grieved that peripheral issues were dividing the church . . . who resisted manmade rituals that were passed down to them . . . who wanted to see the church united by what they had in common. But those previous generations had a lot less freedom than we do today to change things.

In those previous generations, denominations were like so many ships moored in a harbor. They all left, one by one, for the same destination—but each one took a different route to get there. Why? They didn't trust one another for help. So, tragically, they were never within eyesight of each other as they sailed along.

Instead of being one powerful fleet, it was "every ship for itself." Think of what a mighty convoy this might have made—captains sharing resources, offering help and guidance to others when they veered off course. Instead, they each left the harbor with the wrong intention—*to get to the destination on their own, convinced of their own "right way."*

It's time to break free of this curse—to stop the madness—and to find the great blessings that can be had in a unified fleet. The fleet Jesus commissioned in his final prayer.

It starts by giving every concerned believer the freedom to question things without having guilt. We're going to face down every voice that would judge you. And we'll find encouragement from the one Voice we need to hear most.

One-Minute Reflection:

Do you wrestle with a desire to retaliate at Christians who have made you feel "lesser than"?

Is it possible to see controlling church leaders as victims themselves?

chapter 31

TAKING THE FIRST STEP TOWARD THE GOOD THINGS TO COME

We already know that *disengaging from church* is heresy to many. You can hear the objections from hard-liners entrenched in the current system: "Leave God's house? Who do you think you are? Suddenly you've got all the answers for the church's problems? We've done just fine for two thousand years. You couldn't be further off base."

Let me be clear about something. I say this to everybody who resonates with what I'm putting forth in this book—and to any critics and skeptics:

First, make no mistake: The entire scope of my life is to be in relationship with God, the Creator of the universe. I am firm in my belief that Jesus Christ died on the cross for me—for the forgiveness of my sins, and to put me in right relationship with the Father. I want my walk with God to be guided by the power of the Holy Spirit—so that all I do, say, and think is God-honoring, empowered by him, and meaningful to everybody in my sphere of influence.

Second, these are primary spiritual desires. And all believers should have a church where these three desires are respected, encouraged, nurtured, and taught. When doctrinal add-ons or leaders' ambitions interfere with this, they should be called into question by everybody. It's an outrage that so many sincere believers have to play man-inspired games to avoid being ostracized.

Third, I want every person to be given the courage and confidence to question all man-driven aspects of their group. I want nobody to fear that they will be made to feel that their faith is inadequate if they ask questions.

Fourth, I want the church as a body to reexamine its systems. It needs to judge whether that system is bonding believers and encouraging unity—or alienating believers and causing further division. To be an effective body at all—to respond with action and courage to Christ's prayer for his church to be one—our hearts need to be "as one" in all we do. That means we need to renounce the man-driven aspects that cause division, both in the larger body and within the walls of every church. We need to rally around one personage—the one God in three persons, our Creator-Savior-Guide.

In short: THIS BOOK IS NOT ABOUT DISOWNING THE CHURCH. It's not about throwing in the towel on denominations. It's not even about changing the infrastructure; far from it. *This book is a challenge to groups and churches to stop overreaching and micromanaging spirituality—to stop thwarting the work of God rather than nurturing it.*

I'm not telling anybody to walk away from his or her denomination or church, their family of fellowship. What I am telling you is this: Don't be afraid to walk away for a time from a system that perpetuates sickness more than maturity—that encourages division rather than unity—that shackles you with a "form" of godliness that seems right to leaders but denies the true power of God.

Change *Can* Happen
What I'm encouraging is a kind of change that can happen—and already is happening. Change that will benefit individual believers and the church at large.

But first, we need to know what we *can't* change.

I would love to stop the abuses of power, the runaway egos, the selfish ambition—all the toxic, dysfunctional things that go on in the name of God. But I can't stop any of that. And neither can you.

What we can do, together, is *foster an attitude of individuality that allows everyone to take more control of his or her situation*. We have the freedom to say no to all the damaging dysfunction. And with that freedom comes responsibility.

You see, this is also about being accountable for our own actions. It's about *getting up from the table* and refusing to approve of or endure the toxic church sludge—the crap that falls far short of Christ's prayer for his church.

***How* Change Can Happen**
Disengaging from my group was a healthy shift for me. I've already described my old church's culture, where leaders had too much control over people's spiritual lives. The men at the top dictated what spirituality looked like, pronouncing which rituals brought you closer to God and which didn't. Very subtly, they demanded surrender to the code they set up.

As a believer, I deeply embrace the concept of surrendering to God and the Cross—but not to an organization. So I had to banish those control issues from my life. To do that, I had to take a new direction: *to disengage*. My intention wasn't to give the church a Bronx cheer. It was to keep me focused on God instead of a group's man-driven agenda.

Some believers in a situation like mine may have been able to stay in their group. But I'm convinced the majority who experience that level of toxicity are like me. They can't sit permanently under a roof where a power-agenda flourishes. Either their healthy defenses wear down, or their inner resistance keeps pushing their blood pressure up. No one's soul is meant to endure that kind of abuse.

A Contrast with Healthy Churches

Maybe you're in a healthy church setting. Your leaders encourage individual growth in the Lord. They help you identify your spiritual gifts, stoke your passion for Christ, equip you to make a difference in people's lives. They aren't deluded about having rights over your soul. They know God's purpose in calling them as leaders—which is to feed his sheep—and they pursue that purpose.

In that kind of church, I doubt the leaders would have a problem with what I'm suggesting. I believe they would want to keep things simple, as Scripture encourages. They might even prefer to see their denomination drop all nonessentials. I believe such leaders would desire a primary emphasis on C-S-G. And they would encourage your desire to connect with believers outside of your group—to give strength and receive it, in our common pursuit at the foot of the cross.

A healthy leader would be delighted to know you want to make a difference beyond the walls of your church. But an unhealthy leader will fight like hell to keep the status quo.

What It All Leads To

There is no way to make one big denomination for God. According to Jesus' prayer, that may have been the Father's desire from the beginning. But for two millennia we've been too self-willed and adversarial for it to ever happen.

What's the best way to address this reality from the viewpoint of C-S-G? It's to continually speak to the system about its divisiveness. I say, let all the distinctives continue—if they help believers draw closer to God. But no "distinctive" should be allowed to alienate a single believer from others believers.

"Good luck," I hear you saying. I wouldn't blame you for thinking that way. If you look at the big picture, all you can see is a giant ocean liner—and your hand on the tiny rudder. But that's not the perspective to take. Every worthwhile movement has started at the grass roots. What does that look like for us?

It looks like a lot of one-on-one conversations between believers. (My men's group is an example. My wife's women's group is another.)

It looks like a lot of one-on-one dialogues between denominations. It looks like focusing on shared core beliefs and coming together corporately to celebrate them.

It looks like letting go of some familiar traditions—those that don't have roots in God's original plan for his body. And it looks like a C-S-G focus, in our worship together and our encouragement of one another.

Taking a Healthy First Step
Time after time, I've seen something tragic happen to those who don't disengage well. Many have walked away from church in anger—and end up walking away from God. There's a reason for this.

The vast majority of believers sit and stew until they can't take it anymore. They don't have an opportunity to voice their confusion and frustration. So they seethe until they blow a gasket—either within themselves or at somebody associated with their church. That's when they leave the group. And it's exactly the point where deeper trouble for them begins.

While they're disengaged, isolated from other believers, they continue seething. And their anger toward other believers gets associated with God.

These people never find the strength or courage to go back. Over time, they've had too many bad feelings about God, and not enough people telling them, "It's okay. Where you came from is totally screwed up. What you're feeling is real. And God hates it."

How to Begin
I can't emphasize this enough: It's essential that you get your needs met and your wounds healed. And that process takes time. It can be a painful road—but it leads to freedom and blessing.

Tackling this is like any other spiritual endeavor: *It all starts in our own hearts.* Each one of us has the ability to make a change. It starts with how we view and connect with God. How do we pray to him? How do we draw near? How do we know him and open ourselves to him? How do we respond to his Word?

Like it or not, these things are shaped by the roof we sit under each Sunday. In your current place, are you able to say, "I'm being encouraged to place my focus on C-S-G?"

If not, it might be time for change.

Good Things to Come
You already know that I disengaged. Well, guess what? The time came when I went back to church. In fact, I'm there every Sunday. The difference today is, I have a healthier view of what church means to me. And I go home built up rather than torn down.

Here's what I'm telling you about disengaging: Good things can happen in that time away from church. Healthy things. That's the subject of the next chapter.

One-Minute Reflection:

Does your current church encourage you to focus on C-S-G?

If you think it's best to stay in your church, will you have trouble navigating the system's divisive tendencies?

part nine

REFORMING A SIMPLER FAITH

chapter 32

THE MOST POWERFUL WITNESS

You've disengaged from church. There are no more manmade regulations to keep you in line. Now what?

Maybe now you think you'll turn to "Theology Lite." Wrong!

It's tougher than you think to make your primary focus C-S-G. There's nothing "lite" about doing faith with believers from different traditions and backgrounds. Trust me—that's the kind of work my men's Bible study group has been doing together.

The first thing each of us had to do was leave all our groups' luggage at the door. The Holy Spirit is like a bellhop who carries it all away. And that's good, because no human could hold up under the excess weight!

So we set that aside. And once we did, I can't describe to you how refreshing it was to cross-pollinate with each other. We stayed focused on C-S-G. And as we dove into what we really care about, we realized we're not all that different from one another.

But we had to keep it simple. Our fellowship becomes a problem only when a manmade add-on—some doctrine from one guy's denomination—is presented as being essential for everybody. When that happens, we stop, identify what's happening, and take a closer look at what's at issue.

Sometimes this means telling a guy, "Hey, check your luggage at the door." At other times, guys don't even know they're carrying extra luggage. You have to explain it to them.

Dropping Luggage Versus Being Stripped Bare

All this is different from beating a guy's traditions out of him. That's just wrong—and we don't allow it.

We should never discredit somebody's rituals or practices if these give him a sense of drawing closer to God. As long as it focuses him on his Creator, Savior, and Guide, he's not breaking any heavenly laws. His practices may not be essential to salvation—but if they're important to his walk of faith, we encourage it. The wisdom that Meldenius gave us has endured for four centuries now, and for good reason: "In essentials unity, in non-essentials liberty, in all things charity."

Our goal in the group isn't to make everybody's beliefs "C-S-G only." (That would just be starting another denomination!) And our goal isn't to disabuse each other of our traditions. Honestly, that's a waste a time. Our goal is to *find unity as fellow believers and followers of Christ*. That's our focus, plain and simple. And believe me, it requires discipline from everybody.

How does real unity come about? It's when our focus is on loving God—*and* loving each other. It's why Jesus put the Great Commandment in just those terms: "Love the Lord your God with all your heart and with all your soul and with all your strength and with all your mind; and, Love your neighbor as yourself" (Luke 10:27). Jesus said these two things sum up all the Law and the prophets—everything.

Growing Closer to God—in Real Ways
One of the toughest tendencies for disengaged guys to overcome is when their "spiritual strokes" have come from add-ons. After years of conditioning in a denomination, that reflex isn't easily changed.

In a lot of churches—especially the "high-tension" groups—there's a checklist of things you do to be spiritual. Keeping those things is a hard habit to lose—especially when you've been taught your salvation depends on it. The dangerous thing is, over time that checklist becomes a source of pride. But in the end, it's nothing more than legalism. And it does nothing to please or glorify God.

In our group, we talk about growing closer to God. And we maintain that should be about a personal commitment to him—not about performance of any kind. Being in fellowship with each other reinforces that commitment to God. Think about it: If you're in a group with guys who love each other as they pursue the Lord, you won't last long without having the same commitment. You'll realize either you don't care or you need to start caring. But that isn't some manmade pressure we put on each other—it's just a spiritual reality.

Afraid of Our Differences
When I first approached my guys about getting together, all of them were excited. They were interested in having discussions with guys from different groups. A few of us would see each other in the gym and start talking about it. That built up an anticipation. Soon guys were looking forward to celebrating each other's differences under the common love of a Creator, Savior, and Guide.

Then fear set in. Everybody started worrying what would happen when our differences came up. We were concerned about how we would handle those things in each other's presence, face to face. After all, each of us had defined ourselves in God's eyes partly by our church's distinctives. We'd spent years relying on those things for reassurance about *our own* faith. And they'd become embedded in us in ways we didn't know.

But the approach we took simplified things. Everybody came in willing to drop their luggage and focus on C-S-G—and we just proceeded from there. As a result, we made good connections upfront. We began to drop the fluff of our own tradition. And pretty soon the meaning of loving God became clearer to each of us.

It's hard to put a finger on just how this happened. All I know is, getting the manmade junk out of the way helped immensely. Choosing love over judgment was unifying. If we had indulged each other's denominational demands, things would have blown apart quickly.

As it turned out, when we were together, we lost all desire to make any such demands. Those things melted away in the company of loving brothers. There was no reason to "show off your spirituality," an impulse that became repulsive to everybody. Everything was on a level playing field—because there was only one Head of this body.

Back to a Simple Faith

Here's the joy of it all: *We discovered again what it means to have a simple faith.*

Believe me, it was energizing, empowering, and refreshing. We began to be renewed in our love for God and what it means to live sacrificially for others. And nobody had to motivate us. We *wanted* to love God and others.

To me, this is even more remarkable because our stories are so different. One guy had become a Christian only a few years earlier, after his life crumbled in midlife. Another guy had been through a half-dozen wildly different faith-group experiences over four decades—and had landed as a Catholic. Then there's my friend who experienced evangelical life as an African American. And that's just three of us.

The key for us is to keep it simple. We may dive into a book of the Bible for a couple of months. Or, we may read a contemporary book and discuss it. Regardless, we trust each other to bring our unique perspective—because we need that from each other. And we relish getting it, no matter how different a guy's perspective is from our own.

At the heart of it all is C-S-G. And guess what's happening for us? *Our simple focus is helping shape us as effective witnesses for the gospel.* Here's how.

C-S-G as Powerful Witness

Yes, C-S-G helps shape how you present the good news.

If you start with the *Creator*, you're addressing the big question of "How?" *How* did we get here? For some Christians, the Creator is the hardest part of the Trinity to explain—because it's the hardest to prove. Yet I've found it's one of the easiest doors into a conversation about God.

Deep down, everybody has a sense there's something beyond what we can see. Even most atheists agree on that. This came up when Steven Weinberg, a Nobel Prize-winning physicist, debated Christian physicist John Polkinghorne at the Smithsonian Institute. According to Weinberg, "We don't believe in quarks because we've seen them"—meaning, the very smallest units of existence—"we believe in quarks because the theories that have quarks in them *work*." You could easily say the same thing about God. You can't easily explain God. But the theories that include him—which is theology—work!

Every day, I look up at the sky, sun, moon, and stars—and I wonder what started the whole concept of this amazing universe. Then I learned something that helped me get my mind around it a little better. It's called the "Anthropic Principle." This says the perfection of the universe—and specifically the earth—suggests it was prepared for human life.

This majestic globe we live on has the perfect balance of oxygen, water, gravity, and distance from the sun. With just a miniscule nudge in the earth's orbit, the whole ball of wax would be either toast or tundra.

The Body as a Marvel

Then there's the marvel of the human body. Astronomer Fred Hoyle uses a funny analogy to critique the common (or at least atheistic wisdom) of "evolutionary selection"—the theory that says the marvel of the human body is random chance. He says it would be as if "a tornado ripped through a junkyard and a jet airliner was assembled as an end result . . . people would say that's impossible."[1]

In his book *Signature in the Cell*, author Stephen Myer examines how each cell in the human body has a Creator-like signature of its own.[2] Now more and more scientists are coming forward to say we simply can't explain all the various wonders of the body and the massive complexity of the universe.

For that reason alone, I'm continually amazed at how adamant people can be in refuting a Creator's hand in any of this. They insist that nothing we see is from a Supreme Being.

Which brings us back to *a simple faith as gospel witness*. When I'm in conversation with a nonbeliever about the Creator, I just ask, "How could all this have just happened by chance?"

---

1 Fred Hoyle, *The Intelligent Universe* (New York, NY: Holt, Rinehart, and Winston, 1984), 19.
2 Stephen Myer, *Signature in the Cell: DNA and the Evidence for Intelligent Design* (New York, NY: HarperCollins, 2009).

Most people are actually eager to talk about it. As a stranger, I'm no threat to them, so it gives them a chance to marvel on their own over the vast universe. Most end up saying, "Yes, there's something behind this whole process. There is a design. And if that means it's a Creator, I'm okay with that."

The Concept of a Savior

The concept of *Savior* is something most people are eager to agree on, too. It addresses another question every human is preoccupied with: What becomes of us after we take our last breath? The idea of a Savior answers that question.

It also answers a more pressing question we have every day: our flaws and imperfections. Most people I talk with are adult males—and they know better than anyone how imperfect they are! They don't have a problem recognizing sin in the everyday world. The best proof of this is a certain psychological study.[3] It found that men's minds are preoccupied with sexual images between thirty and forty times an hour.

In most of the conversations I've had, people easily see the need for a Savior. They have no trouble seeing they have sins that need redeeming—and a Savior is the meaningful gift filling that need. We're all too aware that we can't live up to even our own moral standards. Trying harder just wears us out and drives home our sense of failure and inadequacy. An external "Savior" makes a great deal of sense—especially if you believe in a loving Creator.

The Concept of a Guide

Finally, we come to the concept of a *Guide* in life. To some believers, the Holy Spirit is one of the most elusive concepts ever. Few have any idea how to explain this third person of the Trinity. When we try, it can sound like a sci-fi film, something that

---

3 Louann Brizendine, *The Female Brain* (New York, NY: Morgan Road Books), 91.

triggers more goose bumps than credibility.

But it's actually pretty easy, once you've addressed the idea of a Creator and a Savior. Why? Because the three Persons in the Godhead answer three basic questions we all have about life:

Where did I come from?

How can I deal with my flawed, imperfect existence?

Where do I find the strength to continue in life?

Here, in a nutshell, is the key to understanding the Holy Spirit. He is our Guide. On a moment-to-moment basis, the God of the universe—the One who created you, and the One who forgives you—has not left you on your own. He is beside you at all times—to urge you to wisdom, to guide you into healthy decisions, to comfort you with hope, and to empower you with love when you feel you have none to give.

That is the Holy Spirit—the living, breathing, eternal Companion who helps us navigate through this life. In a sense, he is the continuation of Jesus' presence here on earth. Only he isn't limited to time and place by a physical body (see John 16:7).

The Goal and the Reality

Our goal is simplicity of faith. Loving God and loving your neighbor are simple matters. In fact, they're the core matters of life.

But that doesn't mean they're easy. They're not. It's why we need a Savior. It's why we need a Guide. They both remind us there's a Creator who has a purpose in all things—One who has the power to shape victories even from our failures.

These three—C-S-G—are the foundations of the Christian faith. They not only sustain us through all things, they're the very fabric of our fellowship.

And that brings us back to Christ's prayer before he went to the cross. You see, as the body of Christ, we're the strongest proof that Jesus truly was sent from God. Scripture says our unity as redeemed human beings is proof of God's love for all of humankind.

That's right—our redeemed lives and sacrificial love are the most powerful testimony to the existence of a Creator . . . to the power of a Savior . . . and to the presence of a Guide. Without our faithful fellowship as one body, the concepts of Father, Son, and Holy Spirit remain just that to an unbelieving world: *concepts*. Abstract ideas.

Is it easier now to see the need for a unified body of believers? For Christ's prayer over his church before going to the cross? For our manmade add-ons not to pervert the profound message of Creator, Savior, and Guide?

These three concepts have to be at the core of even the simplest Bible study group. Because they have the power to transform any human being—and to astonish the world.

One-Minute Reflection:

> When was the last time you "cross-pollinated" with a believer different from you? What was the fruit of that experience?
>
> How is deviating from C-S-G a threat to Christ's witness in the world?

chapter 33

OPTIONS FOR A SIMPLER FAITH? OH, YEAH

You've had a glimpse of our men's group. There's one thing I didn't mention about it that I hope you picked up on anyway: *It's a safe place.*

I can't think of anything more important to guys who need to "do rehab" from a toxic church situation. For some of us, it's been a place to pick up our faith again after setting it aside for a while. For others, it's been a place to rebuild faith, after seeing it battered by manmade crap.

So, what about you? If you've felt the need to disengage from your group, what might be the best place for you to land?

Maybe you need to take a break from the whole thing for a while. You need time alone to try and get your bearings about God. If that's the best scenario for you, and you need permission to do it guilt-free, then consider "permission granted" from someone who knows. Go for it.

Or, maybe you need a group situation like ours—a place where you can engage your faith but be allowed to heal.

Maybe you just want to go to another church. But when

you think about it, you're afraid of repeating past mistakes. You think you might gravitate to one that looks good but could be just as toxic as the last. (Very few "toxic churches" look that way from the outside. Only after spending time in them are you able to sniff out the underlying agenda.)

These are choices you may need help with. Don't be afraid to ask a trusted friend for his wisdom regarding what you need. Or just ask him to pray for you. It goes without saying, involve your spouse. If you've both endured the same kind of abuse and dysfunction, you both probably need help through this leg of your journey.

The Desert Station—Just One Leg on the Journey

I use the word "journey" for a reason. *It describes exactly what your spiritual situation is.* Right now you may be in a place of hurt, confusion, doubt, and even fear. But I assure you: The present darkness is not your final landing place. It's just one leg on the lifelong journey of faith God has for you.

Every major figure in the Bible had this kind of leg in his or her journey. It was true from Abraham to Jacob to Joseph to David to Elijah to Jeremiah to Jesus to Peter to Paul to John. That's not to mention all the major figures in church history—the Augustines, the Martin Luthers, the John Wesleys, the Mother Teresas. And those people are our examples, too.

We're all followers of Jesus. So why would you or I be excluded from such a journey, when these people weren't? God cares about us just the same. And his role as our Guide is to carry us through our wilderness times. He supplies us with hope—you could even call it blind hope—when things are so dark that we forget which way is up.

I'll say it again: *Have trusted friends pray for you.* Have trusted members of your extended family pray for you. You might even approach a friendly local pastor, somebody trustworthy with a good reputation (and who's outside your church sphere). Ask him or her to pray for you. Don't be ashamed or afraid to ask for counsel. Any healthy believer—especially a minister—will want to offer his prayers, help, support, and love.

You need help finding what you need. That's Job Number One for you.

Available Landing Strips
A lot of people are in the same situation as you—a whole lot, in fact. Many of us have been through at least two or three cycles of this sort of experience. For that reason alone, we have trouble reengaging in another round of church. Where on earth do we go? How do we avoid the same old merry-go-round?

Two helpful alternatives have appeared in the past decade. I think of these as options that might fit for some of us. First, there's the *home church* concept. And second, there's the *emergent church* movement. Both have their critics. Yet both offer a different type of service to disaffected believers who desperately want to escape a toxic situation but don't want to lose their faith.

The *home church* concept has attracted a lot of people who endured a toxic church. When people meet for church in each other's homes (or a designated home), it can make all the difference. It provides smaller and more intimate fellowship. To some people, that's more meaningful than anything—especially if their concerns were drowned out in a large church.

Of course, a group's size isn't the relevant issue. Leaders in small groups can be just as controlling (and to a worse degree) as in a large one. Moreover, people can also be just as self-centered in that kind of setting, with less accountability to the community of fellowship.

It's the intent that matters: Is the group all about moving each other toward the Cross—and engaging with nonbelievers as well? Or is the energy focused on maintaining the status quo—preserving comfortability or the group's uniqueness? In that case, the big box has just arrived in a smaller box.

Keep these questions in mind as you look for a healthy place for you and your family to land.

Emerging Opportunities

The second option to explore is what's called an *emergent church*. It's tricky to try to define this movement, as it means many things to many people. One thing I've picked up on is that these groups strive to see the church as a movement, or an organism, as opposed to an organization. They also view leadership as more a matter of example than authoritative control. And they usually have great energy for outreach.

There are a few in my area that have started recently. They use names like The Bridge, The Gathering, and The Refuge—names chosen to imply that they are a communal place and outside the norms of traditional church protocol. They are just trying to bring together those of us who have taken a break from church and are looking for something that feels a little different.

Like the home church concept, the emergent movement has its critics. Personally, I'm all for it, if only because it offers another alternative to the current system.

Both the emergent church and the home church concepts reflect a back-to-basics mentality. Both are about moving away from a corporate structure and focusing on individuals. They might even look more like those first-century gatherings of believers. And for the most part, they operate with sound theology, without self-serving agendas. In short, both concepts encourage a C-S-G kind of approach.

Of course, either movement could end up becoming one more way to "do church differently." In that case, they're just another "flavor of the month," doing nothing to change things. By maintaining the status quo, they risk repeating the dysfunction of the current church system—and that's unacceptable. (In fact, some home churches and emergent churches have already repeated those mistakes.)

But if they maintain a C-S-G-centered momentum, both can offer good alternatives to the disaffected. They're available as useful tools to reignite people's faith.

Maintaining a Love for Church

Okay, I've mentioned these two alternatives for the disaffected. Both are available to most people, except maybe those who live in remote areas. These days, home churches and emergent churches are flourishing in major metropolitan areas and even in small towns.

Now let me offer a qualifier to all I've said here. I love going to a regular church—yes, a denominational church—to enjoy the corporate-body worship. I love hearing a good, traditional sermon that makes me laugh and cry in the same service. I love worship music that reverberates off the walls when groups of believers come together. I love the reality that a larger group of believers can reach out to their community in larger and more impactful ways. In short, I still enjoy many aspects of church as it's practiced in a traditional faith community. I have absolutely no problem with that. In fact, I encourage it.

The difference for me today is, *I don't hand over my individual spiritual authority to a leader.* I don't bow to the add-on demands of a church. As far as I can tell, I don't miss out on a single thing God is doing. I only miss out on the manmade crap!

I'm still involved in people's lives, caring for them as a lay pastor. (This is outside the walls of the church.) I'm even still available to church leaders, if they want me to be involved in an aspect of ministry—but not some program that serves a manmade agenda.

In other words, I'm all about C-S-G. I want nothing to do with a leader's ambition or a church's goals beyond that. Having spent a few years outside the walls—and now, most recently, back inside them—I can assure you, this mentality is the best kind to have.

Please hear me clearly on this issue. I am not saying, "Never join a church." Joining does not have to be bad. It's just a harder step for those who've been badly burned by their church experience. For some, joining may indeed be a matter of "never, ever." But if you feel you can join something and want to, by all means, move on that intuition.

Facing the Nitty-gritty Issues
Maybe you're in a smaller congregation now—say, a home church or emergent gathering. Or, maybe you're involved in a small Bible study group, like the ones Lynette and I lead. The time always comes when your basic differences are going to surface. What happens when you face that dilemma?

It helps that by now, you all know each other. That's been a big help to my group. We've talked across the restaurant table—and my living room—for almost two years. It makes a difference to be up close and personal with six to ten other followers of Jesus when differences come up.

Let's say the issue of baptism is on the table. I come from a Catholic tradition, but I also spent years in evangelicalism. As a child I was sprinkled in the Catholic way, and later, as an adult, I was dunked in the Baptist way. Does one ritual mean more to me than the other? Maybe, deep down, at the seat of my emotions. But even if that's true, I have to be willing to say this: *I will drop any allegiance to one ritual or another for the sake of my brother sitting next to me.*

That's what being in community—close community—has done to my own personal "distinctives." That may sound like bold words to some people. It might sound tame to others. Honestly, I don't know what a statement like that would mean to my men's group. I just know it's the way I feel—most likely because I've spent time at the foot of the cross with them.

Actually, I can't imagine a scenario where I would be asked to set aside a meaningful tradition. If a guy asked me to baptize his grandchild in his family's tradition, I would do it any way *he* wanted. I don't care how far removed from my own tradition it might be—I would be comfortable doing it. Why?

I lose nothing by kneeling at the foot of the cross. And kneeling there is exactly what I'm doing whenever I serve another in a way that goes against my own tradition. I do know this: If I'm kneeling beside a brother, looking up at Jesus, we wouldn't bother asking him how to do baptism! The more important issue to Christ would be that we both *are* baptized in his name. What he wants is our heart. I don't find Paul and Silas getting into a theological debate over how to baptize in the jailer's household. All comers were welcome—and baptized on the spot! (see Acts 16:31-34).

It's amazing how differently we practice these things, based on traditions formed so long ago. We have so many views, and our emotions are deeply wrapped up in them. There's nothing wrong with that. But the question is: What are our emotions toward our brother, who's kneeling next to us? That's what matters most.

It's also why a C-S-G focus is so important, if we're disaffected and looking for a landing place. God has a home for us all on this leg of the journey. None of us has to be alone, scattered through the wilderness.

One-Minute Reflection:

Can you think of an "available landing strip" for your faith? A home or emergent church, perhaps, or even another option?

Do you think you might eventually be able to rejoin a group or church? Why or why not?

chapter 34

A HELPING HAND—FROM PASTORS

There's an important element I haven't brought up yet in this talk about disengaging. It's *clergy*.

Let me say a few words to ministers here. Pastors, I've been telling people what they can expect to happen when they disengage from church. And I've laid out a few options for them. So, what's your role in all this?

I ask because you may be their soon-to-be-former pastor. In that case, hopefully what I've written to this point gives you some insight from the pews.

Maybe you're a pastor in the larger faith community who can provide help. I've mentioned that people may need a minister to help walk them through the aftershock of a toxic spiritual experience. Are you willing to be available to those wounded people?

I know this raises a touchy subject among pastors—the notion of "sheep stealing." It's the idea that one pastor benefits from another's loss of a church member. We need to get past this notion right away. So let's keep it simple: *People need help. Will you take part?*

Involvement and Its Complexities

I know things can be complex. Let's say you know the hurting person's pastor. Helping that wounded person may present a "conflict of interest" for you. If so, would you be willing to refer them to a neutral pastor? Or, better yet: If you're in a good-sized city, there are ministries and Christian counselors who can provide support. Would you steer them toward that kind of help?

Maybe you're the leader of a home church. If so, your gatherings may be full of wounded sheep. You've already got experience in these matters, and there's nothing I can say that you don't already know.

Hopefully, you can draw some encouragement from my emphasis on a C-S-G focus. I've found it provides freedom to many who've been hurt by a church. What these suffering people seem to need most is being able to work through false guilt associated with "failure" at their church experience.

Or, maybe you're the pastor of an emergent church. In that case, your congregation is not only a refuge for hurting people—it's also a magnet for people who are looking to "do church" in a new way. Hopefully, what I've written so far has some appeal to you, for your endeavors. Your kind of church seems tailor-made for people who want something different—not just for themselves, but for future generations of believers.

Watering Down—or Watering Up?

I've been warned by well-meaning friends that by writing a book like this, I might get accused of "watering down the gospel." Pastors, you're trained theologically, so you know better. A C-S-G focus isn't some new theology. It's anything but that.

I'm open and receptive to all criticism, because I don't have a reputation to protect. I really don't care how badly this book gets assailed (and it surely will—not just by well-meaning critics, but by some of the types I've described: arrogant zealots, self-serving power mongers, and corporate ministry-machines. They've all got a stake in maintaining the status quo). The fact is, I have no stake in this at all—except to see believers thrive and flourish as they were created, redeemed, and empowered by God to do.

As a minister, you have that same stake. I don't have to tell you what you're about: the hard work of shepherding, equipping, and leading believers to maturity in Christ and serving a hurting world. I hope what I've written here has encouraged, emboldened, and challenged you.

Mostly, I hope what I've written is a practical help to you in your ministry. If your people can't grow and find fuller, richer fellowship by focusing on C-S-G, then there's something wrong with how it's being done. A C-S-G focus eliminates the manmade elements; *those* are the things that water down the gospel and weaken its power. C-S-G is about restoring that power—power given by the Holy Spirit to transform lives.

Throwing a Lifeline to a Lost Generation
Day by day, an entire generation of believers grows more disillusioned with church. I've already given you the sobering statistics that bear this out. They're leaving church by the droves. They're wandering on the fringes of faith. And some are hanging on by a thread. Others are already lost in the wilderness.

Do this: Next Sunday, look out at all the faces in your congregation. You may see a woman with young children, who is there week after week. Where's the husband, the father?

You may see a man sitting alone. Where's his wife, his children?

You may see a college kid by himself. Where are his parents, his siblings?

Don't tell me your heart doesn't break over this. Don't tell me you don't worry there's no support system for these precious ones' faith.

What has caused their isolation? What's led to the division in these families? Is the lone person sitting there the only family member who's had a conversion experience? I doubt it. You're their pastor, so you know the unlikelihood of that. More likely, it's this: *The missing people did have a faith at one time—but they've opted out of church.*

They're not "backslidden sinners," complacent people who are slacking off. The vast majority are MIA—*missing in action!* They were wounded somewhere on the battlefield of faith, but there was no one to rescue them from enemy fire.

Are they apathetic? Do they just want Sundays to themselves? Not likely. Tell me, who from your church suddenly just decided, "Church is inconvenient for me?" Nobody who ever had a genuine faith comes to that sort of conclusion easily. They've tasted the good thing. And it takes a long, hard battle to pry somebody away from the one thing they prized more than anything else in the world.

The answer is, *people have become disillusioned.* Unhealthy churches no longer speak to people's deepest questions—so they miss meeting their deepest needs. For decades now, too many churches have been busy fulfilling some pastor's ambitions. Or they've oppressed people with add-on demands that are irrelevant to what they really yearn for: a deep, intimate, vibrant relationship with their God.

I've visited dozens upon dozens of churches in the past ten years. I needed to find out for myself if what I've seen and felt is an isolated incidence, or if it's pervasive. Well, there's good news and bad news. The bad news is, It's pervasive—*very* pervasive—for all the reasons I've laid out (the corporate approach, consumerist appeals, a bigger-is-better mentality, an us-versus-them mind-set, etc.).

The good news? *There are a lot of good churches doing wonderful work.* The ministers in these churches are faithful to the task

God has given them. They're not bending to the pressures of "personal kingdom building." Even without an elder board to monitor some of them, these pastors are doing a great job in servant-leader roles. It takes real humility to pull that off. And the people are following their pastors' example. They're maturing into faithful servants of Christ, being a blessing to their community. Pastor, God bless you if you're practicing "good church."

I love the line Rick Warren uses to open his mega-best-seller, *The Purpose Driven Life*: "It's not about you." If leaders led this way, and followers followed this way, there would be a lot more "good church" and a lot less "bad church."

I know. "Duh," you're saying. But the fact is, doing church well in the current landscape is not easy. It's gotten a lot harder because the trends I've mentioned offer so many ways to go wrong. In all my visits to dozens of churches, I've not found a perfect church. There are bad elements even in good churches. And why not? They're run by man. Some have more bad elements than good, others more good than bad.

So, what's the solution? What would it take to build a healthier faith community from the pulpit to the pews?

Simple—and Real—Solutions
I don't pretend to have all the answers. I don't even have a few. Plus I admit, I'm as dirty, weak, and flawed as anybody.

But I can offer one thing that can help anyone and everyone: *a simpler faith*. A faith that struggling people can grasp. A faith that hurting people can find hope in. A faith that drifting people can find an anchor with. A simple focus on C-S-G can be that kind of life preserver to all. It saved me.

I know for a fact, from my conversations with hundreds of men, that people are hungry for this. I've heard most of them pour out their heart with hunger for a real relationship with

God. Those who once had a faith burn to see it reignited . . . to meet in unity at the foot of the cross . . . and to love and serve God together across every boundary—boundaries the Cross has obliterated.

These men may not know how to articulate it, but they have a common rallying cry. God himself has put it in them: "On earth as it is in heaven!" Deep down, we all hunger to see Christ's church as one.

What Do These Men Need to *Hear?*

Each one of these men needs to hear one thing from the unhealthy churches that harmed them: "I'm sorry."

They need to hear a confession—and an apology—from an institution that has brutalized their faith to the brink of nonexistence. The church of Jesus Christ has the power to offer them that apology. This is the same institution that served as a bulwark for God throughout the centuries, battling against darkness as in the Middle Ages.

But the church is also an institution that has perpetrated its own evils. Now it needs to use its power to humble itself before those it has brutalized. It needs to act as the servant God has called it to be. It needs to open its doors to its own, as a shelter and refuge for healing.

So, make that two things the church needs to say: "I'm sorry." And, "Can we start over?"

You see, men need more than an apology. They need a *reset* on the whole thing. And the first order of business is providing them with a safe place to heal. Until they can find healing—and be better able to forgive—they won't be able to move on. They can never reignite their faith.

Pastor, your church can be that kind of refuge. A place where damaged, disillusioned, disaffected men can be in conversation with other men—from other denominations, even—who share a hunger to actually *do something* for God's glory.

What Do These Men Need to *Feel*?

In a word: They need God's touch.

When you've been through cycle after cycle of abuse, you need healing. More than one respected author has written of the church as a hospital. Francine Rivers describes the help of a healthy, C-S-G-centered church after a round of abuse elsewhere:

> Many churches seem to be mere museums for plastic saints, or they preach fulfillment from the world's point of view—a prosperity gospel. This church was different. It was a hospital for repentant sinners; their only blueprint for life was the Bible, which everyone was carrying and most amazing of all—reading.[1]

Author Kenneth Osbeck makes a direct connection between healing and church unity. He celebrates a beautiful hymn that does this, in his book *Amazing Grace: 366 Inspiring Hymn Stories for Daily Devotions*. Osbeck says of the hymn, "The Church's One Foundation": "This is what the local church was meant to be—a spiritual hospital for hurting humanity, never an exclusive private club for self-righteous Christians."[2]

I thank God for the writers and concerned Christians who tackle this subject—the need for recovery from church abuse. One of the most helpful articles I've come across is by Ronald Enroth, in *Discipleship Journal* magazine. In an article titled, "Recovering from Churches that Abuse," Enroth encourages all who've been burned by a manipulative leader or the corporate machine: "Above all, learn to trust God again. Renew your walk with him. Rebuild a quiet time. *Don't give up.*"[3]

Necessary words for the weary and heavy laden.

---

[1] Francine Rivers, *Redeeming Love* (Colorado Springs, CO: Multnomah Books, 2007), 466.
[2] Kenneth Osbeck, *Amazing Grace: 366 Inspiring Hymn Stories for Daily Devotions* (Grand Rapids, MI: Kregel Publications, 1990), 264.
[3] Quoted by Michelle VanSlate, "Burned by the Church", *Discipleship Journal*, Issue 107, Sep/Oct 1998.

But when you've been shipwrecked, you don't always have the strength to continue hoping. You need help. Who will help these wounded, if not you, pastor?

What Do *You* Need to Help These Men?
Now I want to make a request of you ministers: *Consider a new way to do church.*

Consider a focus on C-S-G. If nothing else, consider a focus on the Apostles' Creed. The Creed was agreed on by the early church fathers. Since then, it has endured every age as the perfect summation of the Christian faith. It's been heralded by everyone from Augustine to Luther to Calvin for its unifying quality in belief and fellowship.

John Armstrong writes that the Creed is a powerfully unifying doctrine for every Christian. In his book, *Your Church Is Too Small: Why Unity in Christ's Mission Is Vital to the Future of the Church*, Armstrong said this about the Creed:

> The Apostles' Creed is a dynamic treasure. When we fail to utilize it as a basic guide for teaching the essentials of our faith, we practically invite disunity. Those who ignore the Creed are generally left to focus on truths they prefer to major on, rather than the essential beliefs that have been universally believed and taught by all Christians.[4]

Bam!—Armstrong hits the nail on the head. He says the Apostles' Creed—basically, an agreed-upon statement centering on the role of the Trinity (C-S-G) in our lives—is something every Christian can rally around. When we don't do that, we "practically invite disunity."

One More Important Element
Pastor, consider also open discussions for victims of church abuse.

---
4   John Armstrong, *Your Church Is Too Small: Why Unity in Christ's mission Is Vital to the Future of the Church* (Grand Rapids, MI: Zondervan, 2010), 79.

A lot of guys have questions—simple ones, about faith—that they never got to ask in their old church. For years they've been stuffing these questions down because their toxic church never allowed a forum for honesty. They were made to look spiritually inferior—or even heretical—for asking them.

Here's the irony: It's these very conversations that could lead to glorious unity—*yet they were stifled!* There's a fear from the top that somebody may stray theologically by asking too many questions (ones that may not be easily answered). But most Christians aren't theologically trained, so naturally they have questions about all kinds of things anybody would wonder about.

The challenge is to be able to discuss these things openly while keeping a focus on Christ. It really is that simple. You'd be surprised how many people have never experienced that kind of freedom in a church.

Now, here's my final request of you as a pastor: Talk to men—*about their broken dreams.*

Read on.

One-Minute Reflection:

> Does your church still speak to your deepest questions, desires, and needs as a follower of Jesus?
>
> Pastor, how do you see a C-S-G focus "watering up" people's faith instead of "watering it down"?

chapter 35

IN THE HOUSE OF BROKEN DREAMS

Pastor, here's one more thing to know about the men who may come to you.

Most of these guys are of a certain age. And for most, their dreams have been shattered.

You can't discount this when you're dealing with men who need healing for their faith. I've already expressed my appreciation for John Eldredge, who writes powerfully and tenderly about this phenomenon among Christian men. I won't be able to do him justice here. But, in short, Eldredge speaks of how men have long-held dreams that never come to reality. It's what causes men to end up being "dutiful" instead of daring.

There are a lot of factors involved in this. I'd like to offer an example from my own life.

Going West, Young Man?
Earlier, I described how I left a small Division III college on Staten Island to try out for football as a "walk-on" player at San Diego State, a Division I school. The *Aztecs!* I picked them

as the means of fulfilling my dream to play college football at the top level.

When I got to SDSU, I did okay through the first practices and drills. The problem was, I wasn't big enough to play at my natural position, which was on the line. So the coaches shifted me to linebacker—but I wasn't quite fast enough to excel there, either.

I decided I would work harder than everybody else—to get bigger and even faster, if that were possible. Hard work would be my way to crack the lineup. So I trained like an animal—hitting the weight room, downing protein shakes, running the ropes on the field. And to my surprise, I did get bigger—*and* faster.

But guess what? So did my new teammates—guys who were more gifted, either with larger size or greater speed. When spring football came around, it became apparent what we all could or couldn't do. That's when reality began to hit me: I wasn't going to be the star player I wanted to be.

Facing the Hard Reality

All this time I was taking a full load of classes. I wasn't on an athletic scholarship, so I had limited means. But I wanted to take full advantage of the opportunity that college offered. I had a special motivation because nobody in my family had ever graduated from college. I wanted to be the first.

This meant I had to work at night to pay tuition. I washed dishes till two a.m. Meanwhile, my day started at six a.m. and didn't stop: I had to attend classes, get to football practice, make the athletes' study hall, and . . . look forward to another night of washing dishes. Every minute of the day was taken up with this routine, until I hit the pillow . . . and the cycle started all over again at o-dark-thirty.

One of the classes I took during this time was in psychology. At one point we studied the famous "Peter Principle," which says we all rise to the level of our incompetence. The idea is that we keep working at something until our talent or determination can't carry us any further.

It began to dawn on me: I had lived out the Peter Principle in my life with sports. I was twenty-one years old, and one of my life ambitions—to play major-college football—had come to an end.

I looked around and realized a lot of other guys had faced this same reality. And I saw what happened to many of them: They never finished college. When their core dream wasn't realized, something inside them broke. They didn't have the drive to do college anymore, because their dream had gone bust. For whatever reason, they couldn't summon the purpose or strength to continue school as a non-athlete. So they dropped out without earning a degree.

I was determined not to become one of those statistics. So, what does a guy do when a broken dream becomes his reality?

Broken Dream as Opportunity

It's funny how things turn out. I had just officially quit football, turning in my gear, when I was approached by the school's assistant athletic director. "Hey, Ed," she said, "there's an opening to be our mascot."

Mascot? *Me, a mascot*?

"You know," she continued, "Monty Montezuma."

We all saw the mascot at home games. Monty wasn't just any mascot—not some anonymous chemistry nerd dressed up in a furry suit. No, SDSU's mascot was something different. "Monty" was a big guy—a chiseled guy—who wore a loincloth! He had a headdress and carried a flaming spear—and that was it for the uniform. He roamed the sidelines firing up the crowd with the image of a fierce warrior.

Hmm—maybe I could do that.

"We pay a hundred bucks a game," she added.

I will *do that!* Goodbye, dirty dishes—hello, loincloth.

It didn't occur to me until later: All the time I had spent in the weight room hadn't been for naught. It paid off. Not just any slob could be Monty if your only uniform was a loincloth!

The Truth About Monty

I believe there's a spiritual lesson here for every Christian man. Maybe you should consider it, pastor. Somewhere along the way, guys "believe they can achieve." They think they can *earn* their way to the top level. They've been told all their lives that if they just work hard enough, their dream will happen. This appeals to every man's natural drive. After all, it's the American Dream we've all grown up with: Work hard enough, and it will come to pass.

But there's a problem: *That isn't life.* Maybe Steve Jobs or Donald Trump will tell you it is. And the clichés about hard work are true, in one sense: You'll never attain anything without unswerving determination.

But, pastor, here's where you need to step in. Guys build up all that pressure on themselves for the spiritual life, too. They try to become *spiritual* achievers in the same way. And when it all falls apart—when the Peter Principle kicks in with a sinner who thinks he can "achieve" a super-spirituality—he has no foundation to land on. Like a lot of failed college athletes, he never completes the course.

What the Church Can Be: a Spiritual Hospital for Broken Men

Pastor, you know better than anyone: The church does very little to alleviate this pressure. On the contrary, it often preaches a gospel of self-actualization, the American Dream.

You also know all too well: *Spiritual life is different.* Want to be the greatest, asks Jesus? Be the least.

But guess what, fellow Christian? There is no spiritual perfection. There is no top level of attainment. The top place for all of us? Down below—at the foot of the cross.

Guess what else? All that work you've been putting in? No, it doesn't earn you a sliver of salvation. But it does count for something.

You may think the pain you've been through has no purpose. You may think all your efforts have ended in total shipwreck. And you wonder how the pieces will ever come back together.

Well, remember Monty. See, becoming Monty Montezuma was a way of kneeling at the cross for me. It was a way of acknowledging: No, I'll never be Jesus. But all that work and effort I put in? It counted. How? *It helped me become the man Jesus meant all along for me to be.*

I was the best Monty Montezuma that school ever had. At least I convinced myself I was! (After my era, the university caved to political pressure and neutered Monty into an effeminately regal royal sitting complacently on a throne. Sound familiar, church?)

Pastor, the men in your care still want to be huge, fleet linebackers. And "superman pastors" tell them they can be. But God made very few of us that way. Show us what we can be. Help us be the men God made us to be. And show us the glory there is in that.

One-Minute Reflection:

> What unfulfilled dream do you still have? Did it look any different when you read the story of Monty Montezuma?

> Pastor, how can you help the guys in your church reimagine their dreams as spiritual men?

part ten

**A SIMPLER FAITH
AS A CHRISTIAN WITNESS**

chapter 36

AND OUR WORST ENEMY IS . . .

Our men's group has been together for two years. As I look back over that time, I can honestly say we're being transformed. We're being unified in our love and support for one another.

That's a marvel to me on one level, because we've got such different personalities. It's also a marvel because we come from such different backgrounds, in life and in faith.

But it's also a marvel on a whole other level. That is, *our C-S-G focus is strengthening our witness for the gospel.* I mentioned this in a previous chapter. But it bears repeating here, because it points out a huge weakness in the church. That is, *a focus on nonessentials actually drains our witness to the world.*

The world outside the church has a lot of questions. Obvious questions, including the Big Three I mentioned earlier: *Where did I come from, and what's my purpose? Why is my life so messed up, and why can't I change? And, how am I supposed to navigate this chaotic thing called life?*

Throughout history, the church has been the traditional go-to source. It has provided answers to all the big questions.

But the more de-churched our society gets, the more invisible the church becomes in that dialogue. And the less likely nonbelievers are to turn to the church as a source of answers.

Why We're Becoming Marginalized

Why is the church such a fringe presence in society? One answer is, we're doing it to ourselves. I've shown throughout this book that sincere believers are drifting away from church in droves. In short, *WE are a major reason why society is becoming de-churched.* We're quick to point to a secular culture as our biggest enemy. But we do more damage to ourselves than the world ever could.

You may say, "The church still has the answers. Nonbelievers are just too proud to listen." I'm sorry, but how arrogant is that response? We've already established that nonbelievers aren't looking for "answers" as much as for *people who model truth with loving action.*

How well are we modeling the words of Christ to an unbelieving world? In their eyes, the church falls into one of two camps: (1) arrogant, militant believers, or (2) lazy, complacent softies. (We know them as Newbies and Old Guard.) Neither camp models the Spirit of Christ to the world.

Yet here's the biggest tragedy in it all: *We don't see this as a problem!* The world is practically telling us, "Hey, guys, your most powerful proof of God is your unity. Without that, all the other stuff is meaningless." Still, we don't pour our energy into uniting. We spend it instead on bickering and critiquing each other. As long as we neglect our common beliefs—a C-S-G focus—our most powerful witnessing tool is going to waste.

The Salesman and the Rabbi

Only a few of my airplane seatmates have objected to the need for a Creator, Savior, and Guide. One of those was a rabbi.

This man liked everything I said, up to a point. His objection rose when we came to the topic of a Savior. He said he didn't see the need for a physical sacrifice for our sin.

I brought up the blood covenant that has always been central to Jewish faith. He didn't see that as relevant anymore. In the end, it wasn't Jesus he objected to or how sacrificial Christ's life was. It was the need for a Savior at all. To him, that need had already been historically addressed, through God's blood covenant with Israel. That precluded any need for a Savior—end of story. "Really," he asked, "why would anyone need a blood sacrifice to deal with their sin?"

I was astonished. Didn't this shepherd of souls at least understand man's inability to always make the right choice? The ever-present, continual presence of sin in our lives, plaguing us from moment to moment? Paul had his issue, which he called a "thorn in the flesh." The 'nad affliction alone is a constant reminder to guys of their need for a Savior. And I know the Jewish guys in this man's care were no different. I fear my rabbi friend was in a bit of denial.

I heard another explanation from a different rabbi. It's that there's a constant battle between our good inclinations and our evil ones—and our role is to choose good over evil more often. Sorry, I just can't buy that. Willpower, as a means of consistently overcoming evil thoughts with good ones, just doesn't work—it never has, throughout history! It doesn't allow for human weakness, from which nobody is immune. It's an unrealistic goal, and to preach it is just wishful thinking.

I can tell you this from spending years in men's lives: The subject of willpower has *no-power*, when what men need and want to hear is transparency and honesty. You see, it's truth that sets us free—and the ability to have perfect willpower at all times just isn't the truth. It's as far from reality as you can get!

I know the rabbi was hoping "willpower" would explain

away the need for a present-day sacrifice for our present-day sin. But he wasn't being brutally honest. I left our conversation wishing he had a safe place to explore for himself the need for a Savior, a need that even the Torah talks about. Only a Savior-Messiah's once-for-all sacrifice allows for humanity's continual weaknesses. And only the Cross of Christ—the sacrifice of God Himself—is able to bear the weight of all the world's sins. Both Testaments reflect this truth, in the most realistic fashion.

The fact is, both the Jewish and Christian religions look to a blood covenant from the past for forgiveness of sins. The difference for Christians is that sacrifice was made by *a living person*. It tells us God is involved today, right now, walking beside us as we struggle to control our thorn.

What this rabbi didn't consider was the living, breathing, pulsing aspect of God. He comes to us in the form of the Holy Spirit, our Guide. Even men who don't claim any beliefs know they sin on a daily basis. (They've told me so!) Whether or not they admit it in public, they know deep down they need a Savior.

My exchange with the rabbi was instructive. I realized that the world's objections to the gospel aren't always what we expect them to be. Why? We just don't understand and appreciate how other groups, like Judaism, have set their systems up.

Now let me say this: We can never forget that throughout history Christianity has been forced upon the Jewish people by the point of a sword—not by a Messiah's unconditional love. For two thousand years Jews have been persecuted *in the name of Jesus*. It's a horrible fact we can't ignore—and it's the reasoning behind a common phrase used by some Jews: "A-B-J—Anybody But Jesus." Tragically, this phrase has been burned into the souls of generations of Jews through painful interactions and a disrespect for all they hold dear—even though most Christians don't know what Jews hold dear!

And, sadly, we don't care to know. We only care about where

they fall short of "gospel truth." In other words, we view nonbelievers *only in relation to ourselves*. We don't care to get to know their personal lives, their problems, their concerns and worries, their joys and hopes. If we wanted to know those things—to actually offer a listening ear, rather than critique their lives—they might hear the gospel more readily.

Could it be the *quality of our witness* affects whether they have "ears to hear"?

In his book *Unchristian*, David Kinnaman says that, yes, this is a problem—a big one. Drawing on research from the Barna Group, he concludes,

> There is much more we have to understand about outsiders if we want to represent Christ effectively to this culture. We are at a turning point for Christianity in America. If we do not wake up to these realities and respond in appropriate, godly ways, we risk being increasingly marginalized and losing further credibility with millions of people.[1]

Know what that means, guys? It means *listening to nonbelievers*.

The Salesman and the Atheist

Not all my airplane talks are with churched or de-churched people. It also happens with a fair number of committed atheists. These guys mostly reject the basic premise of a Creator, so the idea of a Savior and Guide are equally unbelievable to them. But these guys are *always* eager to tell me how dysfunctional the church comes across.

I have to admit, listening to their descriptions can be pretty dispiriting. Talk about mountains of evidence you can't dismiss.

---

[1] David Kinnaman and Gabe Lyons, *Unchristian: What a New Generation Really Thinks About Christianity...and Why It Matters* (Grand Rapids, MI: Baker Books, 2007), 39.

Hearing this stuff is like standing before a trial judge as criminal counts are read off: disunity, dismissiveness, character assassination, outright venom. If these were real offenses, Christians could be convicted for life without parole.

The thing is, we have to acknowledge our offenses. Why? *Our witness to the world is at stake.* When somebody like George Barna says so, you gotta pay attention. We can't expect the skeptical world to turn a blind eye to the way we treat each other. Jesus' final prayer in John 17:23 tells us so. He prayed that we "may experience such perfect unity that *the world will know that you sent me . . .*" (emphasis added).

It's not just a skeptical world that stands by watching our folly. It's also a *hurting* world. They're the ones looking to us for *healing truth*. In that sense, our dysfunction and strife become even more tragic. They see what we do to each other—and there's no way they'll turn to a church to find love. Jesus looks like a fraud to them.

God can't be pleased with that.

Fun at Our Expense

Because our problems are so obvious, atheists are having a field day. From writers to scientists to comedians, they're having way too good of a time bashing believers. And they didn't even ask for the ammo we're handing them. We serve it up daily on a silver platter.

Comedian Bill Maher made a documentary ridiculing religion, titled *Religulous*. As I watched it, I spent half the time laughing—and the other half screaming at the TV screen, infuriated by Maher's flimsy case. Sadly, it wasn't hard for him to expose the sideshow-like qualities of the fringe figures and groups he filmed.

As I watched, I had a growing conviction that it should have been a lot harder for Maher to make the case he did. Nobody should be able to ridicule Christians that much without viewers stopping to say, "Wait a minute. I know those people. That's not what they're about. The ones I know are all about loving each other—and loving me! They do the hard work of serving the suffering in our community. I'll listen to them about the big questions in life. This comedian can make all the fun he wants. But I know better. These people are doing something to make the world a better place."

I think Maher is a talented comedian. I just wish he didn't have so much material to work from. That's our bad. Of course, Maher tries to make serious points to discredit religion. So do other high-profile figures—people with growing reputations in the "new atheism" movement, like Sam Harris and Richard Dawkins. I'll address their arguments in the next chapter (and I'll recommend some books that do a much better job than I ever could).

For now, I need to say one more thing about the picture we present to an unbelieving world. Let's return to my airplane conversations. As I've said, almost everyone I talk to is open to the idea of our need for a Creator, Savior, and Guide. But those same interested people run straight into a brick wall when it comes to the church. The number-one objection they have is *having to make a choice to claim a group.*

Get the picture? WE ARE THE PROBLEM. *We are the main hindrance to non-believers' coming to the Cross!*

There are a lot of ways we become a hindrance. First, there's our horrible witness as a scattered, backbiting body. Second, we bring nonbelievers to a membership class instead of to the Cross. Third, when we do present the Cross, it's our denominational version of it, with meaningless baggage that detracts from its power.

The Cross we present to the world should be represented by one element only: the Man hanging on it. The Man who was resurrected from it. The God-Man who has answers for every hurting nonbeliever. He alone offers us truth about *why* we were created, *what* we can do with our broken lives, and *how* he'll personally help us through his Spirit.

It's time for God's people get back to the basics—to gather at the foot of the cross—for the sake of a lost, unbelieving world.

One-Minute Reflection:

> Do you ever listen—really listen—to a nonbeliever's objections to the gospel? Do you dismiss their objections with theology—or do you listen to the life story behind the objections?
>
> How do you feel when someone objects not to Creator, Savior, or Guide, but to the church?

chapter 37

"PLEASE, NOT THE GOD OF THE BIBLE!"

Now, about those critics of Christianity . . .

I'm not the most eloquent guy when it comes to "apologetics." That's the time-honored skill of defending the faith. But I do know wisdom when I hear it, and what makes common sense. And some terrific authors have supplied us with plenty of powerful resources. Some of these are on a basic level, for us Joe Palookas, and others are on high intellectual levels, for those who can handle it.

We all should take advantage of these resources, for two reasons: (1) We need to shore up our own thinking. (2) We need to have a ready answer for the growing number of skeptics who want to do away with all religion.

I wouldn't dare try to defend Christianity myself in a single chapter like this one. But I can point you to few "champion thinkers" in this dialogue with the skeptical world.

"The God of the Bible"
That phrase—"the God of the Bible"—is a telling one among

atheists. No matter what the argument is about, the most common objection from the community of skeptics is, "As long as it's not the God of the Bible!"

The phrase is used by scientists, cultural critics, and plain old atheists—people who'd be happy never to see another trace of religion in the world. Across the board, these thinkers aren't consistent on anything—except their loathing of the notion of a Supreme Being. On any subject, skeptics will consider every "what if" scenario—except one with God in it. They have one common enemy: the idea of a God who has existed historically and will continue to exist eternally.

Together these skeptical voices have been identified as "the new atheism." They claim that religion has only had bad effects on humanity. Some of the more famous books are *The God Delusion* by Richard Dawkins, a scientist, and *The End of Faith*, by Sam Harris. Their unifying concern is, "All religion is bad." But they don't bother to show the great good that religion has been proven to do—things that no other source on earth can replicate.

This tendency to hide the facts tells us something. It's that this chorus of skeptics isn't really interested in knowing *whether* religion is good or bad. They don't weigh its merits and flaws thoroughly or objectively. They've just got a personal axe to grind. In the end, they're not saying "religion is bad" as much as they're admitting, "I don't *want* God to be true." And that's not an intellectual movement—it's an anti-God movement.

Mr. Harris and Intentional Ignorance

Sam Harris admits his anti-God view in his review of a book by Francis S. Collins. Collins is a Christian known for helping develop human-genome science, an astounding advance. Collins writes about this work, as well as his faith, in his book *The Language of God*. Sam Harris concedes a lot about Collins's theories, but, as author Tim Keller quotes him, "Even if there is intelligent design in the universe, it does not have to be the God of the Bible."[1]

At least some atheists have the honesty to admit they're afraid of the idea of a Supreme Being. Tim Keller, a minister and leader in Christian thought, says this is the case with the atheist philosopher Thomas Nagel. Nagel, in his book *The Last Word*, admits his fear of "religion as possibly true." Nagel says if religion is true and a Creator is real, then we need to address the ramifications. If there is an entity behind creation, life and nature, then "surrendering" to that power is the logical choice. And that would be a scary thought for many.[2]

You have to credit a guy like Nagel. His honesty is a help to nonbelievers who want to know how we all got here. They look around at complex, wondrous creation and can't explain what they see. Deep down, they can't accept that this all "just happened," but believe it's somehow the result of a Master plan. Paul Myrant is a pastor who's written a helpful book on this subject, *The Challenge of Evolution*. Like Nagel, Myrant states that a choice must be made about a Creator: "The existence or nonexistence of a Creator has nothing to do with the way religious people behave. The issue is not that religious people have failed to live up to the Creator's standards (which they certainly have). It is whether there is a Creator who has standards to live up to."[3]

Mr. Dawkins and a Quavering Fear of Truth

Richard Dawkins, the scientist who famously bashes religion, states that all faith is blind faith. He says Christian and Muslim children are brought up to believe their religion unquestioningly.

I agree with him about that, generally speaking (though not

---

[1] Timothy Keller, *The Reason for God: Belief in an Age of Skepticism* (New York, NY: Riverhead Books, 2008), 133.
[2] Keller, 123.
[3] Paul R. Myrant, *The Challenge of Evolution* (Mustang, OK: Tate Publishing & Enterprises, 2009), 25.

about being forbidden to question). It's a part of every belief system to accept the basic foundations of that faith. And whatever group you're born into, you're highly likely to believe in that group's tenets, especially as a child.

Actually, Dawkins's point here—about growing up to believe blindly—is what I'm trying to tackle in this book. If we're all brainwashed into our little corners, then we need to emerge from those corners and look at our faith in a more unified way. I can't speak for faiths outside the historical Christian religion—that's beyond the scope of my ability and this book. But for the multitude of Christians with a Trinitarian heritage, it's absolutely essential to do this.

You see, blind faith is a child's approach, not an adult one. There's an honorable segment of Christianity where leaders urge us to explore the realities of faith, not just to accept things blindly. Year after year, thoughtful Christian publishing houses produce thoughtful books by thoughtful Christian thinkers. I'm not talking about seminary leaders, but people whose work is recognized as excellent by the secular world.

I think of the Christian philosopher Nicholas Wolterstorff, who taught at Yale and until recently directed Yale University Press. I think of Garry Wills, the towering Catholic intellectual, who writes on a wide range of cultural subjects and is recognized as one of our nation's greatest minds. There's Francis Collins, whose scientific work I've just mentioned. There's Jon Meacham, the editor of Newsweek. And there's Owen Gingerich, the chair of astrophysics at Harvard, whose Mennonite background helped develop his sense of wonder—a highly inquisitive faith that led him into his lifelong pursuit of science.

That's not even to mention the incredible literary works of writers like Tobias Wolff (*This Boy's Life*) and Mary Karr (*The Liars' Club*), or poets like Franz Wright and Kathleen Norris. These people are recognized masters of their literary forms. All of them, and the rest I've mentioned here, are celebrated experts in their fields—and they all speak of the realities of God. You won't find their names numbered among Christian best-sellers. But they're busy doing the heavy lifting in the intellectual centers of the world.

Yet there's also great stuff being published for the rest of us Joe Palookas. Evangelical presses like InterVarsity Press do a great job of producing theologically astute books for lay people. (They got their start as a college ministry, so they have a history of publishing books to equip people with sound theology on all kinds of subjects.) William B. Eerdmans Publishing Co. does the same. The list goes on and on. If you Google any subject, you'll come up with a mountain of books that address all these subjects and more.

Mr. Maher and the Convenient Avoidance of Logic
When it comes to Bill Maher's movie *Religulous*, it wouldn't take a book to address his arguments. I have to say, I can appreciate Maher's take on the absurd depths of some religious expression. (After all, I'm trying to expose some of the same absurdities in this book—only from the *inside*.) But when it comes to making arguments—man, this guy's research team could use a little help. I can't tell you the number of times he floated something out there and I immediately saw through it—me, Joe Palooka!

Let me give you a "for instance." Maher argues that gods and goddess appeared long before Jesus' time, also claiming to be born of a virgin. According to Maher, these claims make Christianity a copycat religion. In other words, Christian beliefs merely mimicked religions that came before.

I thought that was about the nuttiest conclusion you could come to. I found several of these examples on my own. There's Azura, and there's Zoroaster, the goddess that supposedly appeared in 660 B.C. The mother of Zoroastrianism, she too claimed to be of a virgin birth.

The only sensible response to this is—*so what?* Just because scores, maybe hundreds, of religions make a similar claim, does it mean *none* of them is right? Multiple claims don't negate anything. What it tells us is we need to evaluate them to see which one might be authentic. If nothing else, Maher should have said, "There ought to be further dialogue about this," not outright dismissal. That's just irresponsible filmmaking.

If anything, the similarities of multiple virgin birth stories suggest that one of them *is* right. How? They reflect a timeless, universal human hunger for a true God the world was waiting for.

A skeptic might ask, "But why did God have to come by birth at all? Why not in a puff of smoke? Why bother coming to earth through the birth canal? If you're God, you're not limited to that."

That's precisely the beauty of the Christian faith. We call it the Incarnation—the God who took on human form, that he might identify completely with his creation. He isn't like other deities, who are removed from humanity and make impossible demands of their creatures without ever being involved with them (except to curse or punish). Our God became like us—appearing as the "needed Gift" to save and guide us—in order to fully sympathize with our humanness.

That alone is more than an Azura or a Zoroaster ever did for anybody. Today, both "deities" are afterthoughts. Jesus, on the other hand, is monumental throughout the world.

Combating All Arguments Through Unified Love

I've been talking in this chapter about atheists and skeptics. But I'm no debater. My aim here is to bring it all back to one thing: *what we can do for an unbelieving world by our unity in love.* It's one thing to engage in apologetics. It's another thing to exemplify sacrificial love—and that's something nobody can argue with.

It's been said, "The greatest apologetic is not a well-rehearsed argument, but a wildly loving community."[4]

The only debate I'm interested in is with my fellow Christians. I pose this question to them: "Can we at least get together for the sake of the lost? Can we do "apologetics" by being a shining example of love? Nobody can argue with that. It's what the church potentially does best—loving each other and serving "the least of these"—in a way that only Christ's body can do. And when we're not doing that, our witness is failing. How many will never come to the Cross because we didn't honor our Lord's prayer?"

Now we come to the homestretch of this book. It's time to pull it all together, and ask the question, What now? How do we go forward? And what does that mean for me?

One-Minute Reflection:

> Where on the landscape do you see this statement being demonstrated: "The greatest apologetic is not a well-rehearsed argument, but a wildly loving community"?

> If our God took on human form to fully sympathize with our humanness, why don't we do likewise and sympathize with the world's humanness?

---

4 D.A. Carson, *Telling the Truth: Evangelizing Postmoderns* (Grand Rapids, MI: Zondervan, 2000), 328.

part eleven

PUTTING A SIMPLER FAITH TO WORK

chapter 38

REENGAGING: IT ALL STARTS HERE

Jesus said it. Barna said it. Our best witness to a lost world is our *unity in love*. So, why don't we get it?

Nobody can make a sane argument against people loving each other unconditionally and sacrificially. The world can't dismiss that. And the church can't judge it.

Yet here's what's most important in all this: Our unity is *a lighthouse beacon to hurting people*. When you're in pain, there's nothing more appealing than a loving, caring, healing community. We've already seen it: The church is a spiritual hospital.

So, how do we become this? How do we "do" loving unity?

It sounds like a cliché, but truly, nothing applies more than this simple statement: *It starts with us.* By "us," I mean two groups who can actually do something. First, every concerned lay Christian. And second, the pastors who are charged with our care—shepherds who provide vision and leadership.

I'll speak to pastors in a coming chapter. For now, I want the ear of every Joe Palooka. I have something to say to all the guys who sit next to me on airplanes . . . all the guys who want to reconnect with the idea of God ... guys who want something more for their spiritual lives ... guys who want to make a difference in the world, and who know that God is that difference.

It really is up to us. We—and we alone—must want to see "God's will on earth as it is in heaven." We can't simply leave this task in the hands of the powers that be. Those existing structures can make a difference "as one body"—but they've reduced their focus to mostly denominational concerns.

I'm convinced our denominations have to be shown. They need an example that both demonstrates unity in love and that exposes their lack of it. How is this done? As I've mentioned, it happens through grassroots movements. History shows that's the way most meaningful movements get started—and last.

I've already laid out some ways to do this. We're able to unite in love through small groups, home churches, and emergent churches. If you're reading this, then hopefully you're already on your way. You've decided to make a move.

Maybe you've gotten up from the table ... you've disengaged ... you've sought out an alternative ... and you've begun to heal, grow, and benefit from your courageous move. I tell you, God sees your movement. And he is faithful to meet you on your difficult but rewarding journey. Let me offer you a few words of encouragement as you continue forward.

1. You are reconnecting with God.

I know this idea sounds strange to a lot of people. You mean, someone can make a deliberate decision to *leave church*—in order to *connect with God?*

Sometimes extreme situations call for extreme measures. If you were compelled to make this decision, your situation was extreme. You counted the cost of simmering on the back row of your church, where you were dying for months, maybe years. And it took guts for you to leave.

It takes just as much guts to do what you're doing now. That is, to kneel alone before an audience of One and bring your struggles and sins to him. You do it because you know he alone has the power we all seek: to forgive our sins. Never forget that.

Yet let's be honest. The thought of such times of intimacy with God are intimidating to some guys. It was much easier to make a silent confession while sitting in a church pew. Now it's just you and God. There's no way you can B.S. your way through the conversation that's going to happen.

Let me tell you how it has gone for me. Maybe I can offer something about what you might expect.

On "Day 1" after my decision to disengage, I woke up relieved—and free. That positive feeling has not changed. When I go to bed at night, I can't wait till morning comes. It's another new day—a time to connect with God afresh. I was still in pain from my toxic experience, of course. But that became secondary to the joy and freedom I felt. Nowadays, as I realize I've been granted another day, I'm excited to get started.

I begin connecting with God each morning with a three-part conversation:

Part one: I tell God, "Thank you." I thank him for another day. I don't take this lightly, as I lost my only sibling, Michael, to a heart attack at way too early an age. I then launch into a thank-you list of the many blessings I enjoy: my marriage, children, job, home, health.

Part two: I tell God, "I'm sorry." I go into a confessional list, singling out the ways I've fallen short. (In any given twenty-four hour period, I never lack for a lengthy list.) Then I ask for forgiveness.

Part three: I ask God, "Guide me." I need him for everything the day will present. And I express my desire for him to be near throughout it all.

It's that simple. I start my day with, "Lord, thank you. I'm sorry. Please, be with me." You can't get more basic than that. Do you see the pattern? *It's all* C-S-G!

I'm convinced there are no more profoundly important prayers than these. In saying a simple "thank you," you're stating your *purpose for living*. You're acknowledging your *Creator*.

When you say, "Sorry, forgive me," you're stating your *hope for life*. "I know I have a *Savior*. He has all power to cleanse me. His resurrection has set me free from all power of sin and death. And that sparks new life in me."

When you say, "Guide me," you're stating trust in him. You have confidence that your *Guide* is faithful to lead you into wisdom for all things.

Thank you. I'm sorry. Guide me. That's it.

Beyond this, everything else is a "faith aid"—things to help you personally connect with God. There are no other obligations or necessities.

"Faith aids" can look different for each of us. You may gravitate toward devotional books with short readings, like "Our Daily Bread." Tools like these remind you of God's Word, including his promises to you.

Or, maybe you play a worship CD because it draws you closer to God. Or, you tune into a Christian radio station.

Maybe you're a journaler. If so, try writing down a prayer at the beginning of your day. It can make your meditations more concrete and purposeful. Plus, at the end of the day, you have a record of your prayer. You can refer to it to see how God chose to answer you. Also, weeks or months down the road, you have a record of your spiritual journey and of God's faithfulness to you.

Obviously, there are any number of ways to start the day. What's most important is that by doing this, *you're reconnecting with God*. And for people in our situation—believers who are *disengaging in order to reconnect*—it's crucial to connect when the day begins.

Coming out of a bad faith-community experience, we're subject to all sorts of condemning thoughts. You may already be dealing with judgment from your old group. Or you may be prone to self-condemnation. That's only natural. You've probably spent months, maybe years, wrestling internally over your faith community.

God is there for you at the beginning of every day. And he wants you to know those times of torment are behind you. His Spirit, whose very nature is to bring "times of refreshing" (see Acts 3:19), comes to heal and restore you.

2. You are reconnecting with other believers.
Okay, I admit it—I'm a normal guy, like you. And the thought of "seeking out others" can induce an anxiety attack.

In all seriousness, this may be the hardest thing of all when you're recovering from a bad faith-community experience. My advice here is, start out slow. Seek out maybe just one person—somebody who'll listen and not push you too far past your comfort zone.

Friends like this are rare, I know. But I can assure you, there are more people than you think who are willing to do this for you. You could approach them by saying, "Look, I'm going through a painful time right now. I really need an ear from someone. I know I'm a bit of a mess—and I promise not to entangle you in my stuff. But would you be willing just to listen? Maybe meet for coffee every week or two, until I get through this?"

You may know somebody else who's in your situation—someone trying to reconnect with faith after a bad experience. Like you, they're also in a tender place and need help themselves. Don't be afraid to seek them out. Together you may be a mess. But I assure you, when God sees you "gathered together," needing healing, he is there in your midst—and he's faithful to meet you.

Whoever the other person is, getting together will bring a much-needed element to your recovery: fellowship. As you begin to open up, you might incorporate something from your devotional time. Maybe share a worship song that means something to you, or something from your daily reading that morning. Or, if you feel safe enough, and it's appropriate to the conversation, share a thought from your journal.

You'll be amazed at how good you feel putting words to all the things you've had buried inside. Not only that, expressing your needs to another believer is important. It establishes a bond that God wants for us. If the other person is from a different faith group, all the better. You'll cross-pollinate on the things you have in common—namely, C-S-G—and that will keep you grounded.

The key here, though, is that you talk to another believer. It's one thing to talk to God about it all. It's also important to share with someone who can walk with you and help bear your burden. If together you're too much of a mess, you can always seek help. It's out there—I know, because I found it.

3. You are (gulp) reconnecting with a faith community.

Okay, enough for now. This subject—returning to a faith community—demands a chapter of its own. And it's coming up next.

Stay with me, soldier. We're going there—together.

One-Minute Reflection:

> Do you see how *disengaging with church* can be a step toward *reconnecting with faith*?

> What "faith aid" might help you most as you try connecting with God at the beginning of each day?

chapter 39

OLD PLACE OR NEW?

After two years together, the men in my men's group are getting what we need. We have true fellowship. We open the Bible and talk about it. And we're helping each other in everyday life, offering personal support on all kinds of levels.

As I write this, one of our guys is enduring some heavy, heavy hardships in his family on several fronts. We're there for him, and he knows it. We're just looking to ease the burden of his trial however we can.

All to say, we're getting stronger. We've benefited from a C-S-G focus. And as we go from strength to strength, guess what's happening? A hunger is growing in each of us to see Christ's body united. One by one, we also wonder how we might reengage with our respective faith groups.

I'm all for it. If we disengage just to stay in our own little circle, we won't be pleasing God any more than wayward denominations do. We've only added to the problem by further "splintering" Christ's body.

That's not to say we won't always need our small group. I

think most of us will. But the main purpose of our group is to let God heal and restore us. We want that, because we want our energies going toward his purposes on the earth. And one of those purposes is to see a church united in love "on earth as it is in heaven." We want to help paint a picture of loving unity that draws in the world with amazement.

Some guys in our group wonder what to do about reengaging. One of the most common frustrations they voice is they have no idea how. When they look at their old church, they see nothing has changed. So their first question is where to go to try to reengage with believers.

Other guys actually want to return to their old church or faith group. They've tasted God's healing, and they want to be a positive force "back home." The question for these guys is whether they can effect change—or, short of that, just stay healthy themselves.

All of this calls for reflection. Some of us have personal issues that led us to toxic environments in the first place. We may have gravitated to a charismatic preacher because we liked the value that was placed on God's Word. At the same time, we weren't aware of how much we wanted a strong leader to make hard spiritual decisions for us.

The upshot is this: You may easily detect one red flag but be blinded to another. We all have blind spots—we're flawed human beings, after all. That's part of the healing God wants to do in us on this leg of our faith journey.

A New Place or Your Old One?

Let's talk about what happens if you choose a new faith community over your old one.

You may need a clean slate for your own psychological health. Seeing people from your old church can trigger old feelings and reopen wounds. If you're in a place where few people know you, you have the chance to start anew. That's what Lynette and I did. We haven't regretted it.

If you choose this route, I suggest you sit in the back row and soak everything in. If you get involved in ministry too fast, it can cover up a lot of hurt that still needs healing. You can always "turn up the volume" later, when you start to feel yourself again.

Just be cautious. The reflex to "do," rather than letting God pour out his love on you, can be a coping mechanism. That doesn't mean it's unhealthy. In fact, you may be just naturally wired as a "doer." In that case, God's healing may come to you while you're in your most natural state: involved in hands-on ministry.

In either case, it's a good idea to keep up to date with your "share buddy," the person you rely on during your healing period. They can offer good reflections on how they see you progressing.

Going Back to Your Old Church Home

Let's say you choose to go back to your old church home. For those who can do it, I think it's a wonderful choice.

Be warned, however, going back can be an emotionally-charged experience, and not for the better. We're emotional beings, and we weren't meant to separate our spiritual lives from our emotions. Thus, everything in your past can be a trigger, no matter how much healing you've done. Just be prepared for it.

And you'll need to establish some good boundaries. Before, you weren't in control of your church situation; the reigning dysfunction was. "It" dictated to you whether you were up to snuff spiritually (usually according to the leaders' demands). Now you need to be in control of your own spiritual growth, rather than leaving that to church leaders. As soon as you start to sense otherwise, it's definitely a red flag. I encourage you to partake in the opportunities for growth. Just don't let the powers that be have the final say in everything.

On the positive side, you may be received warmly by old friends who are still there. In my mind, that's the best-case scenario. You have a safe place to land, because they know you and care for you. Hopefully, things will have changed enough that the environment is no longer toxic but truly a "spiritual hospital."

Of course, there's always the possibility it's just not the place for you. You may still be carrying too much baggage from your previous experience. Old resentments may rise up, or you realize you went back with the idea of intentionally changing things. That's a great motive, on the surface, but it's usually not a wise one—especially if you're an army of one.

If any of this describes you, and you're determined not to give up on your old church, let me offer an additional option. Consider getting counseling. Talk sessions can help you get past the disappointment and anger you're feeling. It can also give you a sense of control that you might not have otherwise.

In fact, counseling may be necessary even if you don't go back to your old church. I sought it out, and it helped me immensely. As I mentioned earlier, it took almost three years for me to come full circle in the healing process. I had to deal with a great cycle of feelings—from powerlessness, to anger, to revenge, to sadness, to grief, to consolation from God. Dealing with all those emotions was a part of the healing process. And I couldn't skip any of them. Otherwise, I would have short-circuited the fullness of God's work in me.

It's good to remember, too, that God's economy is different from the world's. We can't always effect healthy change in others. People don't change simply because we're able to convince them of something. It comes about mainly because *it happens in us first*—and they see it and want it. If you can go back to your church as an example, a picture of spiritual health, that's wonderful. But you can't be an example if your own spiritual health is at risk.

Avoiding Perfection in the "Church Search"

Let's face it—there is no perfect church. Anywhere. We all need to know that going in. Especially those of us who have been burned. There's never going to be a perfect home for our faith until we get to heaven.

But that doesn't mean we can't "be as one" now, to honor the Lord's desire. And working toward that oneness is simple, as I've laid out in these last chapters. Lay Christians, we can begin to do our part.

Now, pastors, it's your turn. Let's talk.

One-Minute Reflection:

> Maybe you're considering reengaging, but with a different church. What blind spots did you have in your previous church experience?
>
> If you want to return to church, but your blood pressure goes up just thinking about it, would you consider getting counseling?

chapter 40

"CAN YOU DIG IT—PREACHER?"

Working toward oneness.

Pastor, I have to ask: How do you feel when I bring up that phrase? I suspect it brings up all kinds of feelings: fear, risk, hope, futility. Or, more likely, indifference.

Actually, I understand that. How could something as vague as "unity among Christians" be anywhere near the top of your agenda? So many other urgent matters call for your attention every waking hour of the day. Sermon preparation, visitation, elder squabbles, budget crises, grumbling in the pews, the needs of your wife and children. I've already mentioned my respect for those following a calling into ministry. For that reason alone, my hat will always be off to you.

Yet something is happening outside your church walls that you need to be aware of. One way or another, it's going to affect your ministry in the months and years to come, if it hasn't already.

Next Sunday, when you step into the pulpit, take a look at the young people in the pews. How many are there because they've genuinely accepted their parents' model of faith? Teenagers, college kids, young career people—for many of these, the old way just isn't working. The younger generation is highly skeptical of the way things have gone. They know they don't have to accept it blindly. They think our generation has listened to "the man"—and where has it gotten us?

Your own silent majority
Young people aren't the only ones who've been disaffected. It's likely church isn't working for the boomers in your pews either. But they won't say anything. Why? Probably because they've been through several church cycles in their lifetime. At this stage, they're worn down from always "seeking and not finding."

They started out hungry in the faith, and over the years they've wanted to grow. But as the decades have passed, they've seen church leaders exchange one model of "doing church" for another. To these boomers, it's a tired old game. How could they get excited about the next "new phase" the church promises? They've seen it all before. And they're not going anywhere, because they're tired of church-hopping. They despair of ever finding "it." In short, they're done.

All these earnest people—young and old—are the reason why alternatives sprang up in the past decade. I've mentioned the popular grassroots faith movements: home churches, emergent churches, independent small groups. On one level, they're happening because people need something more.

Yet make no mistake. The people flocking to them aren't just dissatisfied shoppers who can't find the right "shoe size" in a church. They're hungry souls crying for healing . . . wanting greater purpose in their lives . . . desiring more intimate fellowship . . . seeking meaningful ways to pour their lives out for God.

These movements should be reason enough to tell you, "Be alarmed, Pastor." But there's more. I'm convinced there's another driving reason behind these movements. They're happening because of a deeper impulse—something that's rumbling inside all of us.

A Yearning from the Spirit Himself

What is this impulse? It's simple: *God's people yearn to be one.*

Deep down, it's unsettling for any believer to be part of a body that's so fractured. And it *should* be unsettling! Paul says the Spirit groans within us. I can't help wondering if one of the reasons for this groaning is our fracturedness, our divisions, our judgment toward each other.

If we've been made alive in the Spirit, we shouldn't have to "drum up" a desire for unity. It should be part and parcel of who we are. Deep down, we actually *want* to connect with others.

In a recent chapter, I pointed out to lay believers the simple ways they can take part. Now I want to talk to you, pastors. Maybe the best approach is to recall an old movie. It might be one you remember.

"Can You Dig It?"

Maybe you saw *The Warriors* when it came out in 1979. It's a "what if" movie about hundreds of gangs that run New York City.

One gang in particular, the Riffs, has the idea to unite. Their leader, Cyrus, calls for a twenty-four hour truce so the gangs can gather, hear each other, and strategize.

At the movie's center is another gang, the Warriors, from Coney Island. They're few in number, and they get behind Cyrus' vision.

When the big meeting takes place, Cyrus explains his vision. He states that together the gangs could rule New York City. He points out the futility of fighting over their small, insignificant pieces of turf. So he challenges the gangs to unite, channel their energies, and work for the good of the whole. If they could just do that, there was plenty to be had for everybody. But divided, they would end up annihilating each other.

His speech is met with rising waves of applause. It ends in a crescendo, as Cyrus shouts repeatedly, "Can you dig it?" Everyone catches the vision.

Then a rival gang comes into the picture. One member stands up, takes aim and shoots Cyrus—and all hell breaks loose.

The rogue blames the Warriors for the chaos. From that point on, the Warriors are moving targets. They have to make their way across New York City, dodging deadly rival gangs to get to their home base of Coney Island. It's a tale of vision—and survival.

Hopefully, the parallels to denominations here is clear enough. We all should be uniting for a common goal. But instead, we're fighting for our little patch of turf. And we're forced to dodge each other's bullets along the way.

Here is my point in bringing up *The Warriors*: The average Christian will always look to clergy to provide vision. Pastor, this means your people take their lead from you. Where will you lead them?

This issue of oneness in the church isn't a neutral one. We're all players in this. What will you do?

Putting Down Swords

I see healthy church leaders as being like Cyrus. They'll call for unity however it might be achieved in their sphere. They know best how their flock can benefit from mixing with other believers.

But for unhealthy leaders, the call to unity poses a threat. It means a loss of power and control. Unity would deemphasize their autocratic leadership.

The time has long since passed for pastors, churches, and

denominations to put down their swords. Pastor, I ask you, Are you wielding one? You may not think you are. But, please, take an inventory of your ministry. What's your track record on this issue of unity? What do your sermons reveal? What do your actions—or indifference—reveal? Does your life show you to be more against unity than for it? In what areas do you demonstrate unity for your flock? Where do you encourage them toward it? Active or indifferent, how do you explain your ministry in terms of Christ's final prayer for his followers?

Now let me offer you something bold. *Your vision for unity can be prophetic.* It can reach across lines in ways you never thought possible, to touch those outside a Trinitarian faith. I personally have seen relationships bridged between Christians and Jews—*in my own family!* That's right. The Christian-Jewish divide is one of the most difficult to cross. Yet when my niece married a Jewish-raised man, it worked out for God's glory.

Because of their differing faiths, the couple decided to meet in the middle by attending a Messianic Jewish temple. This is a Jewish community that accepts Christ as the Messiah. What a wonderful, moving blend of Old and New Testament doctrines. Now my niece and her husband enjoy a richness of faith undreamed of before they married. Neither feels they've compromised anything they believe. I believe their marriage will only lead to more blessings.

Let me throw out a thought here not just to pastors but to all believers. It doesn't matter what group you grew up in: You have a tendency to cling to what you were taught as a child. Simply put, that's your reference point for God. But if you're nonpracticing today—if you feel stuck because you can no longer digest all you've been fed—I hope you're gaining hope by what I'm stating here. No matter what your background—Jewish, Catholic, Protestant, Witness, Jack Mormon, whatever—if you're disengaged because of confusion or conflict, I want you to know something: You have a God who mercifully offers you simplicity. Come now to your Savior-Messiah—to C-S-G—who is found at the Cross.

What Every Pastor Can Do

If you lead a church or ministry of any kind, I'd like to make a suggestion. It comes from my years on the front lines of lay ministry. It's simply this: *Curb your "pursuit of excellence."*

In other words, stop working to make your church "the best there is." I'm sorry, but that's a worldly pursuit. Besides, your standard of excellence and God's are two different things. If you don't think so, just compare the fruit of your standard to God's. Your standard breeds competition between churches. It encourages people to "compare and choose." It also builds an invisible wall of separation between believers. But our calling as Christians is to tear down walls, which Paul says is the power of the Cross.

You may object, "But every guy is competitive at some level. That's how our church became successful." It's true many men are built to be competitive. But I'm not talking about "taming men's nature." God's Word does talk about competition—that we're running a race, one we're meant to win. But we're not running it *against each other*!

Besides, none of our natural strength counts in this race. To win it, we need the strength of God himself—that is, his grace. Thankfully, by what he achieved on the cross, he offers us that strength daily.

Here's another suggestion. Next Sunday, after you step down from the pulpit, ask yourself four questions:

> Would this sermon hold up if I preached it at the foot of the cross?

Did my message keep faith simple, based on a C-S-G focus?

How did this topic bring my parishioners closer to other believers?

How would this message help a Joe Palooka in his daily walk of faith?

I bring up this last question to purposely refocus on men. I have my reasons for doing this. I think you'll be able to relate.

One-Minute Reflection:

Do you see why, deep down, God's people yearn to be as one?

Pastor, what parts of your ministry work for or against the unity of all believers?

chapter 41

SIMPLE—FROM CRADLE TO ETERNITY

I've told you about my parents' visit to the evangelical church Lynette and I attended. I spoke of how excited my mother was at the idea of renewing her faith commitment by publicly confessing Jesus as her Savior and Lord. What I didn't describe was my father's reaction that day. He wasn't excited about it at all. He decided to back off from the experience.

That was my dad. Like a lot of men of his generation, he didn't show a passion for religious things. He supported my mother and me in our early devotion to Jesus and our passion for church. But mostly he kept his thoughts about faith to himself. That doesn't mean I didn't try to pry them out of him at times, especially when I was a young zealot. But he wasn't the type to talk about those things at any length.

It was years later that I found out the depths of—and the reasons behind—my father's reticence. I told you early on that he was a painter by trade and that we lived on a block filled with other working class men and their families. Well, the hazards of my father's trade caught up with him. For all those years, he worked with lead paint as well as products containing asbestos. As happened tragically to so many others, his life was going to be cut short.

My father had been retired only two months when he received the terrible diagnosis. Not long after that, death began its approach. I was with him at one point during his last couple of weeks. It was then he brought up the subject with me. I was sitting with him, talking with him about eternal things, when he confided, "Eddie, I never knew what to do."

I knew what he meant. He had always believed, but he never knew how to act on it. And he was ashamed to ask. "Son," he asked me, "what do I do?"

Immediately, it came to me exactly what to give him. "Dad, it's simple," I said. "So very simple. Remember the thief on the cross?"

I told him the story from Luke 23. It's the moment when Jesus is hanging on the cross, at the end of his life. Two thieves were facing that death also. They hung on crosses on either side of Jesus. Neither of them seemed to have a religious background. One thief cried out in frustration, challenging Jesus to rescue them and himself from the situation. The other thief rebuked him, saying they deserved their death sentence but that Jesus didn't.

The humble thief then did something that is talked about to this day. He asked Jesus, "Remember me when you come into your kingdom."

It was raw belief. This thief did more than most "believers" in Israel had done during Jesus' ministry on earth. He believed.

This man knew Jesus was about to die. Yet he still believed Jesus was the Messiah—the Chosen One, God Incarnate—who was greater even than death.

The fading Savior of the world promised him: "Today, you will be with me in paradise." *That* was the bottom line for this man, said Jesus. Not crucifixion, not guilt for his crimes, not even death, which was moments away—but life eternal.

Jesus saw in this man what no one else did: *raw faith*. It was raw hunger, based on raw need—and it led to raw belief. The thief may not have ever been religious—we can't know. But what he said was the single most sensible thing to the ears of the God of the universe: "I believe in you."

My dad listened. Over the years, he had been confused. He'd grown up Catholic, then he got a flavor of evangelicalism when Lynette and I took him and my mom to church. Afterward, my parents tried a Baptist church in their hometown. Then Dad ingested several more flavors through television. Knowing him, all this probably confused him about which group was "more right."

I leaned over my dad and gave him a big hug. "Pop, if you haven't done it already," I said, "You need to tell Jesus you believe in him. Start by telling God you're thankful for sending his Son. And that you accept the free gift of his sacrifice for your sins."

I told him he could do this alone, in a private moment with God. I believe these commitments are so deeply personal that they should be made alone, in private. When you think about it, it's the most intimate moment of life—between you and your Creator-Savior.

It was a sweet, sweet moment for me. And I wanted that same sweetness for my dad—alone with his God.

A Benediction for Dad

A few weeks later, I got the call. He was in the last stages. I jumped on a plane back home to New Jersey, hoping to make it before Dad passed.

My parents' neighbor picked me up at the airport in Newark. On the drive to OverlookHospital, the neighbor said Dad had started to spiral down quickly. "But I got to speak with him, Ed," he told me. "And he said to me, 'I'm ready to go home.' He told me he had his talk with God, and that he knew he would be with him 'when the time came.' Do you know what he meant by that?"

I smiled. Dad had had his moment with the One who matters most. The One who says to everyone who calls on him, "Today, you will be with me in paradise."

I did make it to Dad's side. I was there when my father took his last breath—and I had the privilege of praying him home.

That has been the best moment of my life. I knew that my dad had his moment on the cross next to Jesus. And he was home.

Simple—from Cradle to Eternity

That was all it took with a guy like my dad. One conversation about a thief's *raw desire for God*. Suddenly, a lifetime of confusion over God and religion became crystal clear—because the truth was simple.

Pastor, brother, sister—*that's all it ever takes: a simpler faith.* The gospel *is* simple—as simple as C-S-G—and it's meant to be shared in the simplest ways. Always.

So, Dad—this is for you. And it's for all the men like you. It's also for the many Joe Palookas out there like me—men who are looking to love, to give, and to worship with all our hearts—simply.

I say to every man reading this, Yes, you have a place in God's kingdom. And every man like you has a place in the pews. The Lord wants you there—shoulder to shoulder with the next guy, to give each other all you have. That's been his desire since his final prayer on the earth.

Ed Galisewski

My Own Final Prayer

After all these pages—all the stories and conversations I've led you through, all the many reflections on *a simpler faith*—my prayer is this:

> That by the grace of Jesus Christ, God Incarnate, *every pew will be brought closer* together.
>
> That *our real care for each other* will extend beyond the secret confessional of a hotel room.
>
> That all the *barriers of our own making* will drop with a thud—and we kneel together humbly before our Savior.
>
> That the *simple truth of the Cross* will reach every disaffected man long before his deathbed.
>
> That God blesses you with the redemptive truth of his crucifixion and resurrection—through which we have the privilege of knowing our Creator, Savior, and Guide.
>
> May he renew your purpose in life, as his beloved creation.
>
> May he guide you into serving others sacrificially and unconditionally, in the example of our Savior.
>
> And may you extend to others the comfort with which you have been comforted—by the Comforter Himself.

God made you. He has redeemed you. And he has a purpose for you. It really is that simple.

One-Minute Reflection:

> What simple approach to the gospel would you take with a loved one on his or her deathbed?
>
> When you reflect on the endpoint of life, how does it shape your thinking about the need for *a simpler faith*?

Ed Galisewski

www.ingramcontent.com/pod-product-compliance
Lightning Source LLC
LaVergne TN
LVHW041539070426
835507LV00011B/823